Credit @Cressida jade

JOE PYLE SNR - JOEY PYLE JNR
LIKE FATHER LIKE SON
A Journey of Minds

To James
Best wishes

Dedicated to my father My lord and my Best friend

JOSEPH HENRY PYLE

1935 2007

LIKE FATHER LIKE SON
A Journey of Minds

Like father Like Son – A Journey of minds is the joint work of joe Pyle snr and jnr. Both keen lovers of poetry, this book is a compilation of both poem books Looking at Life and From Villain to verse-maker.

This book also contains a few unknown stories as well a few excerpts from the script of the motion picture currently in post-production about the life of Joe Pyle snr.

There is also extra poems that never made their poetry books, one of which is a poem snr wrote for Ronnie Kray when he was in Parkhurst prison.

I have also included a few chapters of my time in South Africa, a fun time which turned very dark.

It is a tale of my life which few people know but I have included it into this book as there have been talks about the possibility of a future movie being created from it.

CRIME –criminal or gangster? Those are funny words which to me don't really have much meaning. What is a fucking criminal? You read books about Al Capone who shot everyone in some far-off world called Chicago. But this is London so people link the Krays to those words.

Straight-goers use words like these when they look down their noses at you and label you. The Krays weren't criminals to me, they were just three brothers who wanted to get ahead in life and made use of their talents. So, they killed someone, what's new.... half of our so-called heroes have killed people!

Murder! That's another one of those words, if I kill someone let's say just one person then I am a murderer but if I join the army and kill a hundred people then I am a soldier! What is the bigger crime? To kill one man, a man who might want to kill me or to kill a hundred nameless men just because it's my job!

Soldiers even get a priest or holy man giving them prayers before they go into battle.

if you weigh this up then you soon discover that the world we live in is not a fair world, the odds are stacked against you, it's a world of hypocrisy and double standards and a world where the real criminals do not come from the poor parts of town.

Behind every so-called crime there is a reason behind it,

Some people murder because they are sick, some because they enjoy it, some do it for survival while some do it because there is no other choice.

In these pages you will find some of things you read very cold, very to the point but mostly you will read what it is like to live in a world where few can judge.

If you are one of those people who like to stick labels on people then throw the fucking book in the bin! It's not for you!

But if you have heart and a soul then hopefully you understand the meanings behind the verses.

The underworld is another word which some people like to label us, so if we are the underworld then who the fuck is the over-world, everything has an opposite so where is the underworld's opposite?

I think for the sake of this book I will call that dark mysterious world I inhabit the underworld then. So, what is the underworld?

To me it where I live, it is my domain, my life and the place where I feel most at home, from the day I was born I was introduced to what is the 'Top table' of British crime.

Some say I am a crook! Some say I am their father, others their pal and some say I have saved their lives, whatever I am, I live life the way I want to live, always have done and always will.... Am I good or am I bad... I guess you'll just have to decide for yourselves?

To Mum & Dad I know you always did your best
my children and the newest member of our family,
Little Nate Joseph
and also
Some of the people I have had in my life and lost.
Joseph Henry Pyle, Catherine & Arthur (Arnie) Pyle, My
dear sister Sue, Uncle Den, Alec Steene, Roy Shaw,
Ronnie Kray, Charlie Richardson, Charlie Kray, Peter
Tilly, Terry Marshe, Johnny Nash, Danny Simms,
Peter Brayham Wilf Pine

**

'It's a Dog eat Dog world, always has been,
and sadly... always will be.... BUT THAT DOESNT MEAN YOU HAVE
TO BE A FUCKING DOG!'

Mitch Pyle Warren Joe Pyle jr Alan Pyle Teddy Bam Bam
pic Credit; Jocelyn Bain Hogg

Forewords

That smile,
That glint,
That sparkle in his eyes.
Joey was only a little boy when I was introduced to him by his Father and my Friend, Joey Pyle.
A little boy with sticky out ears and a Smile......That Smile.
He can break your heart with a look and then stitch it back up again in a moment with just a Smile.
He had an old head on very young shoulders and he carried it well.
Surrounded by big, powerful men, Joey seemed at home.
For me these men and his Mum Shirley were the foundation of the Man Joey has become.

A Good Man
A Goodfellow
your Friend

Raymond Winstone
From across the River

Clive Black (Best pal & Godfather to my son Manny Pyle)
MD of Blacklist records inc.

When Joe asked me to write a forward for his book of poetry I thought why me and what can I 'say'?
You see when it comes to Joe and his world I never 'say' anything.... it's better that way! ☺
I do often whisper to Joe my thoughts on life and try to give him advice from an angle others close to him may not dare to – you see what Joe is to me is just 'honest' he says it as he sees it and holds zero back.
He is 'loyal' beyond the call of duty and over the last 20 years he has been my closest friend. The one I can rely on – no questions asked.
Charismatic and unreadable Joe is a man of many layers......peel back the tough exterior the gangster, you get the family man, the friend, then the creative side flourishes, he writes, acts and dreams of making big things happen ...he is a man of great depth and of many dimensions.
His heart is so big that he spends all his profits making sure all those around him are 'sweet'...even the local hospitals and kids charities get 'looked after' anywhere Joe puts on an event...looking after the locals is in his DNA...he comes from a stock where your turf was everything and the people who lived there needed to be looked after...Joe Snr was a massive figure in my life – full of wisdom , he said in a sentence what most took an hour to say but the best thing about getting to know `Joe Snr was one day he said to me ' meet my son you will get on great' ...and we really did and always will do – Joe and I are friends for life thanks to Joe snr..
You feel safer in this mad world just knowing that Joe Pyle is your mate and on your side.
Now Joe - I hope you got some good rhymes in this book of yours and for Christ sake use spell check!!! ☺

G-d Bless
Clive

Jimmy White MBE (The peoples champion & Very good friend)

When joe asked if I would do a foreword for his book of poetry I didn't hesitate to say yes. I have known his father joe snr for all of my life. Being a south London Tooting boy which was his father's stomping ground we became good friends and from that friendship I got to know Joe jnr who is around my age. We have had some blinding nights out together and share some very good friends. I wish him all the best with this book and hope everyone enjoys it.
God bless and good luck with the book Joe, your Pal Jimmy White MBE

Ori Spado (My Dad in Los Angeles)
Beverly Hills, California

I first met young Joey when he was a young man and instantly I saw what his character was. I have watched him grow into a Man. Not just kind to his friends and family but he is there for them. But most important is his intellect of analyzing a situation, getting the facts and then makes his decision. If I were to write everything good, I can write another book. Those who know him then I must say hold your head high and be proud as there are few real men left and Joey is certainly one of them. In the years since his father and my dear Mate passed Joey has become my third son and I, am proud of that. although there is a big pond between us I wake every morning knowing if I needed him he would be here for me and me there for   him, in a fast changing world I can say from my heart I know this with confidence and as I learned in my life the only ones I can count on like that is my family and Joe is my family. LL&R   look in the dictionary and you will see Joey,s name. I love you Joey.

Freddie Foreman

I have known young joe all his life. His book will be a big success of that i am sure. His dad would have been very proud.

Wilf Pine (family friend and author of Englishman and the Mafia)

What can I say about this highly respected family? I have known 'Junior' as I call him all his life, he was a cheeky little sod and has been a lot of other things in his young life but he has always been loyal to his family ways and his family friends. His father was my dearest pal, the Boss of Bosses who even after we lost him ten years ago, I think of him every day. Junior is like his father, a man of honour and truth and someone you can rely on when you need to rely on someone. He is my best pal's son but I have no hesitation in calling him one of closest pals.

Good luck with the book Junior, I know just like everything else you put that mind to, you will make a success of it.

And kiss those lovely kids for me.

God Bless Wilf.

Mark Morrison (return of the Mack)

To my brother Joe jnr, my old manager and most trusted friend, Never stop being you, Joe. Brothers till the end of time

Mark (Peace)

Shirley Hine (Mum)

My son joey, I've Known him for fifty years, I should do I'm his mum.

Good Luck with the book joey I'm sure you will be doing more this is just the start of something new   Your life is in the boxing   Nobody knows the time and effort you put in to it. You are so caring and you wear your heart on your sleeve. A family man and a true gent … knock you down and you will always get back up and try harder in whatever you do. Good luck joey and get that film out there, My joey.

Mitch Pyle (My Brother)

What can I say about this man that has not already been said? Except I have been a part of this family for 20years now and was taken in by Joe Pyle sn. And the best thing to come of out this life is a man I can call my brother Joe Pyle jr. a man of Respect. A man with Honour. A Business man in many things. A man who stands by he's family no matter what it is. A man I call my brother. I love you and will always be by your side. Love loyalty & respect.

Alan Pyle (My Brother)

Good luck with the book Joe, you're my older brother and have always been there for me no matter what the cost. I know you are always trying to look out for me and as brothers we are always there for each other, no matter what comes our way.
Love ya
Al (HMP Wormwood Scrubs)

Dave Courtney (Uncle Dave)

Hello people.

Firstly, may I say what an honour it is for me to have the privilege of writing a forward for a book that ain't a gangster orientated piece of literature. And for it to be for someone that happens to be more than a very very good friend of mine is just excellent for me.
I have read through this book a number of times now and I must say that the more I read it the more I learn. I feel it is a real piece of wisdom from someone's mind that knew what he was talking about, and it shows in its truthfulness and honesty.
Sir Joey Pyle Snr, my mentor, also wrote a book of poetry whilst in prison and would have been very proud of his son's first publication which is also a book of poetry.
It's well worth a read and if you are intelligent enough to appreciate the knowledge and heartfelt emotions from someone's mind that knew what they were talking about, you would call it a classic.
So I am asking you, not telling you, just take my word for it that this book is the fucking bollox.com.
Dave Courtney OBE

Veronica Richardson (Wife to Charlie Richardson)

Charlie first introduced me to Joey's mum and Dad over 25yrs ago. Little did I know then that they and Joe jnr would become lifelong friends. Joe was a cheeky rascal then and we have watch him grow into a very handsome successful man. I know his Dad and my Charlie would be proud of today. I am honoured to be part of his and his beautiful families' life and I know he will only go upwards. Good luck with the book Joe xxx big hugs xx

Steve Wraith (The Geordie Connection! A man of many talents who is very dear to my heart)

Joe Pyle has been a good friend of mine for over 25 years now. We may live 350 miles apart but we are only ever a phone call away from each other. This man puts his life and soul into everything he does and is well respected the length and breadth of the UK. His talent knows no boundaries as this book shows. Good luck brother....

Anthony Spado (Brother from the USA)
OCS Entertainment, Los Angeles CA

Well first of, congrats on penning this verse book Joey! All I can say is anything Joey creates or speaks about truly comes from an authentic place. They broke the mold when you were born and you have achieved more success than most can imagine in a lifetime.   You're my brother from another mother across the pond. May you have all the success with this book and many more to come. One love!
Anthony Spado

Stephen Sayers (Staunch and loyal friend to me and my father)

From one author to another I wish you all the luck in world with this book. You're a chip off the old block and your Dad would have been very proud.

Christian Simpson. (Kindred Spirit)

Mr Joe Pyle is not only a very respected individual within the boxing industry on a global scale but he also is a truly gifted writer with the ink of a pen.
Proud to call him a friend for now, well over 20 years.
Wishing Joe, all the best of success with this book of poetry, that will have been written from the heart.
God Bless from Christian Simpson.

Alan Paramasivan (Always been family & as Old School as they come)

From Villain to Verse…aka Cheeky Wee chappie to Poet and after reading the enclosed you will know it! Trust me he hasn't gone all soft on us. Far from it, he has quite openly and very frankly and 'at last' put pen to paper allowing us an insight to a very entwined detailed life, following in the footsteps of his late Father, in as much as being very respected amongst powerful people in London's underworld as well as being a straight and upfront business and loving family man. He has many, many stories to tell, some that he can't, the others he shares first hand in this extremely clever and entertaining format. Joey Junior aka Joey London has travelled from boxer to now boxing manager, mixing with everyone worth mixing with and will, knowing him as I do, be powerfully successful in the fighting promotional world as well as the literary business bringing you amazing entertainment. If you get the opportunity to ever meet Joey, you will immediately realise he is a man of intriguing depth. That added with creativity and humour allows him naturally to translate his knowledge into story telling. I've had the pleasure of knowing Joey Junior since he was a wee cheeky chap from a school boy, always looking as if butter wouldn't melt with that beaming smile, through his mischievous teenager years ducking and diving all over London and now having joined the adults in the fifties club he is completely focused on giving everything he does true value and significant meaning, all of which you will all now be privileged to witness as he puts pen to paper. His late father was a very, very dear and close friend of mine and I'm certain that he is looking down very proud indeed. To me Joey is family and these my personal comments about him and his work may well be bias but I am a man who doesn't suffer fools and I can hand on heart tell you upfront that you will be pleasantly moved with what you are about to read.

Much Respect and Love, your pal Al.

Jocelyn Bain Hogg (Author of The Firm and Family books)

I have kind of grown up with Joe. I was there in 1997 with my camera photographing my first book The Firm and him being, well him. He's never changed in all these years. Always the same keen intelligence and wry, dry sense of humour. It was great to find someone in that new world who was my age and didn't judge me. Joe was always as straight as it got and that too has never changed. Somewhere Joe has a destiny to fill that is all his own and now is his time: he is a rare one and I am proud to be his friend. I greatly look forward to literally this new chapter.

Michael Coleman (The Original Gentleman & one of my dearest pals)

It is with absolute pleasure and an honour to o be asked by my very close and best friend Joe to write a little about him for his new upcoming poem book. I've known Joe a number of years now and can honestly say Joe is a king of kings and born leader. He comes from an extremely highly respected family
and after the passing of his father in 2007 has done his late father and all family and friends proud by filling the empty shoes and grasping the reigns tightly. Joe has a heart of pure gold and is highly intelligent and superbly knowledgeable! He looks out for absolutely everyone and cares deeply and loves all his family and friends. Joe is shown love and respect wherever he goes and is polite and respectful to everyone. However, God help anyone who makes the mistake of trying to wrong him or anyone who is connected to him as Joe will not take kindly to this and they will pay for their mistake! Joe will stand by your side come rain or shine and I will do the same for him and we're all family and hold deep love and respect for each other. Joe is one of the few old school left now and knew all the fellows and will put anyone right if they're getting their facts wrong and can and does tell so many stories of old and will have you listening like your life depended on it. His humour is second to none and always puts a smile on your face. I'm

honoured to have Joe as a best friend and brother and will always love him as such, Michael Coleman

Michael Biggs (Former business partner & son of legendary Train robber Ronnie)

Many years ago on a very private conversation during a so called "underworld" event Joe told me about his poetry, in a macho dominated environment that we were in to have Joe talking to me about poetry was unconceivable. After looking at Joe for a few seconds to see if he was just pulling my leg I could sense he was trying to reach out to me with a different side of him, this was no longer Joey Pyle Jr. the son of the legendary Joe Pyle Sr. as I was no longer Biggs Jr.

We were two fathers speaking of the importance of nursery rimes and how to educate our children and make them the best literate humans we could through the love of reading. This was in total juxtaposition with the setting we had around us of flat nosed, aftershave smelling, cropped headed hard looking blokes.

Since that conversation our relationship was never the same as I have looked at Joe as someone who is more in touch with people's spirituality and what they have to offer. Joe is hardly ever seen to have a softer side to him.

Many who read this may not believe the words above however look past the surnames and past histories and they may find that especially in this case - the book cannot really be at all judged by its cover.

Michael Biggs - March 2017

Cream (USA Rapper & family to the bone)

I met joe Pyle around 15 years ago, I had an instant attraction to his aura and his attitude to life, Joe helped me grow as a man and as an artist, and I'll always be grateful for the guidance he has shown me, he took me under his wing like a family member would, and that is what we became...family. His loyalty is 2nd to none, his business knowledge it's fascinating to watch grow. I was born to be by this man's side for life. He has always shown me the real Joe and I wish him the best of luck always. This book will be one hell of a read. Love you Joe

Teddy Bam Bam (One of the inner-circle & obviously a man of very few words!)

Good luck with book Joe, TED!

Terry Barrett (Some call him weird but a 'Goodfella-friend of mine)

THE DAY THAT I MET JOEY PYLE, HE HAD THIS SWAGGER AND CERTAIN STYLE,
NOT SURE WHAT I THOUGHT AT FIRST, TO BE HONEST I THOUGHT THE WORST....
BUT IN TIME I HAVE GOT TO KNOW,
I HOLD HIM HIGH AT FIRST WAS LOW, BUT NOW WEVE GELLED, HES A SUPER GUY, HES PRETTY COOL HES PRETTY FLY.... I DID NOT KNOW HIS DAD JOE, THE TYPE OF GUY I WOULD HAVE LOVED TO KNOW, I MISSED THE BOAT ON THAT MY FRIENDS, AND THIS IS WHERE THIS POEM ENDS.... T....
XXX

(Sonny) Joseph Michael Pyle (My eldest son)

To my father, the man who I respect most, the man who has raised me and a great man. I am very happy to have you as my father.
JMP

Manny Alexander Pyle (My second born son)

My name is Manny Pyle and I am writing this for my father, Joey Pyle. He is a very hard working man, he always tries his hardest and an inspiration to me. Love you dad.
Manny.

INTRO

Born naughty?

Is anyone really born naughty? Can your genes dictate what life has in store for you?

If such a statement is true, then surely, I must come close to the mark. I was born into a family where records can be traced to the old bailey criminal courts in central London back to the 1700's!

The first Pyle documented at the old bailey was back in 1777 when Paul Pyle was found guilty of stealing handkerchiefs in Paddington, Paul Pyle was sentenced to transportation to Australia.

In 1812 john Pyle was sentenced at the old bailey for theft with violence and was publically whipped at the corner of Caledonian road and Pentonville road in front of a crowd of over a thousand people. The following year John Pyle was arrested and found guilty of burglarious breaking into the shop where like his grandfather he was sentenced to transportation to Australia for seven years.

In 1857 another John Pyle was found guilty of stealing suet from a butcher's shop and just like his relatives he was given seven years' transportation to Australia.

So, that is just some of my family, just some of the early records we have found but of course I did not know these men. Let's move forward a couple of hundred years to the turn of the last century.

My grandfather Arthur Pyle was one of five brothers and was also a twin to his brother Joe. They were born around the Kings Cross area of London which was on the borders of London's east end. It was a harsh area where crime was rife and men had to fight to get any kind of respect.

My grandfather was a quiet man but was very well respected around the cross; he would use violence as a last measure but was very good at winning when it mattered. His twin brother Joe was completely the opposite, he was loud and somewhat flash, when they would go out and do a warehouse or ping a safe my granddad would save his money, Joe would go out and buy a new suit and waste his money on clubs and girls.

It is funny but many people say that my father Joe snr took after his namesake Joe while many say I inherited the quiet thinking side of my grandfather.

My grandfather met the love of his life Catherine Gray (my father's mum) she was a tough east end woman whose mother came from the tough streets of Glasgow.

My grandmother was the toughest person I have ever known, she was ruthless in her adoration of her family and couldn't stand outsiders, some of my earliest memories of her is when she used to say to me, 'Joey, never let anyone take any liberties with you' and another saying of hers was 'Be wicked! When they know you are wicked then they leave you alone'

My grandmother was from Irish and Scottish catholic heritage and whenever she got the chance she would always sing the Irish rebel songs; Kevin Barry was her favourite song and for as long as I can remember she would sing it at all the family gatherings. It's funny as other kids my age was being taught to sing nursery rhymes like hickory dickory dock! I was taught to sing rebel songs, like 'shoot me like an Irish soldier' it was a strange up-bringing, a different up-bringing but to me it was normal.

I suppose I was born naughty!

Must have been in the genes or something, the saying go's he was a born villain, or a born crook, I was definitely born something like that, can't see it any other way really, it was my destiny as sure as I was destined to grow my first tooth.

I certainly wasn't destined to become a lawyer or a banker or some other nine to five mug. (as we called them)

I wasn't born into poverty nor was I born with a silver spoon stuck in my mouth, I was middle class, I lived in a middle class area, went to a middle class school and had middle class mates but something was always different with me, I just didn't fit into anywhere, I made plenty of mates as I grew up but I lost them as soon as got them as I discovered their morals and ways were different to mine, morals and codes that were drummed into me from the time I could walk.

My upbringing wasn't particularly hard or strict but it was very much different, I was taught at school about all the usual educational things but then I had another education at home, it was like a secret society to me, a romantic, fun and forbidden way.

Everything about my home life was different from my friends' houses, their fathers and families were plain, ordinary, boring,

My father's family and friends were 'tough guys' they looked tough, acted tough, drove flash cars, wore flash suits, carried lots of cash and dominated any rooms they walked into.

I wasn't born the wrong side of the tracks or any of that old bollocks, I can't stand all that crap about how I was born potless, sure we didn't have much but honestly, I couldn't give a fuck about what I didn't have, all I cared about was what I was gonna take.

There were three certainties at my birth, I would break the law, I would go into boxing and I would sometime go into prison. All three were as natural to me as growing my first tooth.

It was the oxford and Cambridge University of crime

My Nan would say, 'He's a boy! ... Boys are always little devils.'

So, it was no surprise I grew into what most people call a rascal, to me it was natural... I was right and everyone else was wrong, I loved the clannish ways of my family, to me they can never be wrong and even now where I walk in the world of the businessman the wolf within can never be tamed.

Rules
Never ask who it was phoning
Never talk too much
Leave the room if friends came around
Mind my own business
Never repeat anything that I might overhear
Never ask questions.

In the next few chapters you will hopefully find someone who has strived all their life to break free from the confines to which I was born into. This isn't just another crime book. I have not done large amounts of porridge or been involved in a headline crime, yes there have many many times that I have broken the law and yes there has been times I have thought about being what people call a gangster.

For me my life has been about trying to make it legit, trying to be secure and doing everything in his power to make it other than be a crook.

**

Just one moment of madness
Can rescind a lifetime of moments

INTRO 2
Joey Pyle – My father

To write my story I feel I need to begin with a brief chapter about my father, although there will be many mentions in the chapters ahead, I want to break down some of the myths and try to give you a true reflection of the man. So many things have been written about him over the years – Don of Dons, the Boss, the main man. If you pick up nearly any villain book somewhere inside the book you will come across the name Joey Pyle, Books written by The Krays, Freddie Foreman, Tony Lambrianou, the great train robbers, Paul Ferris, Dave Courtney, Charlie Bronson, Howard Marks, Wilf Pine, Roy Shaw, Lenny McClean! All of their books mention him in some shape or another.

My father passed away in 2007 after a three-year battle with motor neurone disease and there isn't a single day that goes by where something or someone doesn't make me think of him.

to me he was my dad, the man I could trust and the man I looked up to. In my life, there are only four people who I truly lookup to, Jesus Christ – Mahatma Ghandi-Cassius Clay and Joe Pyle.

I am not saying he was a saint or divine but he was everything I have inspired to be. He was strong and he was fair and for a man labelled as a villain he had an amazing empathy for those who he shared this world with.

My dad lived in two areas in his life, Caledonian road North London and Carshalton on the fringe of South London. Over the years, he remained friends with people on both sides of the water.

People say he is a hard act to follow but those who say that don't know me or my father, one of the main things he instilled into me, is that no man should follow another man, you follow your heart, you follow the way you believe is true, he spent his entire life living this way …. So have I.

Early life and mischief

My poor mum was over the moon when she gave birth to me in 1967, tired from the birth she was surrounded by friends and family all keen to get a glimpse of new born son. The room was full of flowers and dozens of telegrams. Congratulations from around the world. Reggie and Ronnie Kray, Freddie Foreman, even a telegram from the USA which said 'Mazel Tov, Meyer and friends' which was sent from Meyer Lansky and another one from Chicago outfit boss Sam Bataglia.

On the first day of me entering this world I was visited and held by Ronnie Kray, Jack the Hat McVitie who robbed a chemist or something and brought with him half a dozen black sacks full of baby clothes and nappies. Tony Baldesare, a notorious armed robber who was best friends with my father. Peter Tilley, another well-known south London face and Oliver Reed the famous actor.

So, I wasn't even a day old and already I had been held by some of the most fearsome gangsters in London and I was dressed in stolen clothes!

That night my father went out with his brother Ted and his pals and drank the pub dry, then at six in the morning dad turned up at the hospital with Peter Tilley and Tony, still drunk and struggling to lift a huge new television they had got as a gift for the nurses.

So, that was first couple of days on this earth, I was too young to remember of course but one of my earliest memories was a year later when I was on the run! Yes, one-year-old and I was hiding out in Italy with my mum dad, sister and Johnny Nash and his wife and Peter Tilley and his wife.

The reason was because of the arrest of the Kray firm, my father and John were in business with them with different bits and bobs so when the twins were nicked my dad and John decided to have it away until they found out just what was happening.

That's an old villain way of life, if someone gets arrested who you are close to then you get away until you find out just what exactly is going on. I cannot remember much about it but my father told me that he and John didn't know at the time if they were going to 'get a pull' the Krays arrests was all over the papers and Scotland yard were really banging the drum about cleaning up London from organised crime, so in their minds it was better to be safe than sorry.... So, one and a bit year old and I was on the run!

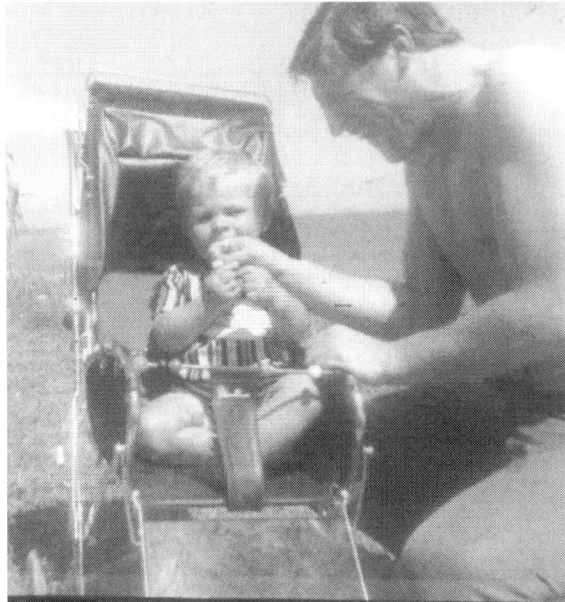

Me and well-known London villain Johnny Nash lying low in Italy.

Early life.

We moved to a two bedroom flat in Southey road Wimbledon when I was around seven-years-old. Southey road was just off the high street and I can remember mum taking me to the shops and some of her friend's houses. From what I can remember of Wimbledon I really liked it, I can remember it being very clean and respectable. It was like another world from some of the places I had lived like Stoke Newington in the East End and Kings Cross where I had stayed with family in my young life because my father was in prison or on remand. Kings cross come to think about it was great fun also. The Second World War had finished just twenty-five years or so earlier and much of the east end in those days still had hazardous ground where unexploded bombs lay buried. I remember once as a child when I was staying with my nans sister aunt Maggie, me and a couple of pals used to travel the canals down to kings cross where we would play in the barren land and explore the dozens of old tunnels they had there in those days. One day we found this large metal case at the bottom of an old abandoned building, there were holes in the roof and everything was falling apart. On the ground level, there was old bits of wood everywhere and we used to gather the wood to make a fire. One day when we were ripping up the floor we found this metal case which was three quarters buried in the mud, we found an old rag and started to clean it then found some writing on it. There was an older kid with us, Billy, one of my cousins and he quickly told us all to run. At first, we thought it was the police or the railway security so we just followed and ran till our lungs were bursting. Once we finally stopped I asked my cousin what was wrong and he told us that we had found a doodlebug bomb from the war. We all laughed and I remember making a suggestion that we go back and get it and then put it outside the doors of the local bank at the Angel in Islington. Later that night I hatched my plan and the next day we would borrow my uncle's wheelbarrow and return to the abandoned building to get the bomb. I didn't have a bloody clue how heavy it was or that the reality of three kids picking that up was an impossibility, nevertheless, we were going to get it, take it to the doors of the bank and throw stones at it and hope it blew the bank up, we would then run into the bank, steal the cash and make our getaway to the canals where we knew that no cars could follow us.

That night I can remember hardly sleeping because I was so excited, at around eight in the morning I remember my Uncle Len calling me down the stairs. I walked down and saw that there were two policemen standing in the hallway. My first thought was about the bank job we had planned so straight away I just clammed up and looked at the floor.

Uncle Lenny then looked at me hard and said, 'where was this bomb Joey?' I shook my head and said I did not know, Lenny asked me again and I just said 'I ain't saying nothing!" the policeman then laughed and knelt down, he grabbed my arm and I can remember him grabbing it very hard but then when I looked up he smiled, "look son, you're not in trouble, but we just need to send someone in to find this bomb, someone can get killed if we don't find it"

I looked up at my uncle Len and twigged that my cousin had told his father that we had found a bomb whilst playing. Uncle Len had then called the cops to report it as just like any responsible father he didn't want kids playing around where there were bombs.

"Joey, you are not in any trouble, just tell them"

"Why don't you ask Billy, he is the one who told you about it?" I replied. talking about my cousin.

"Billy is at school." Lenny replied

"Well I ain't saying nothing, Nan said never talk to the coppers!" I answered determined.

"Joey, this isn't talking to coppers, it's just helping them to keep the area safe." My uncle Len said.

"Well I ain't fucking helping them!" I snapped back.

I was then sent to my room and the policemen went to Billy's school where my cousin told them where to find the bomb.

Later that night I can remember having a terrible row with my older cousin where I called him a grass and we had a massive punch-up in the room. My uncle Lenny came upstairs and grabbed hold of both of us and I can remember him grabbing me by the scruff of the neck and pushing me onto the bed, he was furious that I called his son a grass.

"Don't you ever say that about family!" he shouted at me.

"Family don't tell tales!" I said back to him.

Uncle Len then sat down next to me and grabbed my hand, he looked at me and told me he knew about my plans to blow up the bank, he was trying not to laugh and then said that his son was not a grass, he didn't tell the police he just told his father about the crazy plan, he wasn't trying to get me in trouble but just trying to save my life.

"In my book that's a fucking grass!" I can remember saying.

My uncle Lenny shook his head, Lenny was an old-school villain and was famous in the underworld as being what was called a 'safe-blower' he was one of the best and he knew the old ways like the back of his hand. Lenny was good friends with my grandfather Arthur Pyle and together they had 'screwed' dozens of establishments, Uncle Len's claim to fame was being the first man to ever use gelignite to blow a safe in London. Together with my grandfather they would rob the 'Gelly' from the stone quarries and then use it in their work. It was a very dangerous thing to use, too much and you would blow the building up, too little and you would not blow the safe but you would make enough noise to alert everyone nearby.

Lenny was not a big man but he had a very intense character, he could look at you and without saying a word you just knew that you were in trouble, Lenny grabbed me by the face hard and looked at me.

"You listen Joey, a grass is the worst kind of scum in this world, and you never ... ever call someone that unless you know for certain that that man is a grass!"

It's funny but from that early age I still keep those words close to my heart and to this day they have never made me wrong, there have been many many times in my life where people throw cheap accusations around, I don't get involved in gossip, I hold my own views and my own opinions and if anyone ever says to me that someone is a grass then I want to see proof! That way of thinking comes from all those years ago, me finding a Nazi bomb and my dear old uncle Len teaching me a lesson in life which had made me some lifelong friendships.

In later years when I was in Belmarsh prison I wrote this poem, some of the other cons copied it out and stuck it on the walls, I can remember the screws pulling me up one morning saying I was causing a disturbance on the wing! I laughed and said that I thought prison was about reform? Well I am writing poetry so isn't that fucking reform?

THE SLAG

You sold out your friend to save your own skin
Your name is now soiled to you and your kin
You betrayed the trust; you sold out your soul
Your scheme was successful; you scored your sick goal
No one respects you, even your pals the police
Your life now is running, you'll never sleep in peace
I watched you in court lying to my face
Now I'm in prison, preparing my case
How could you do it? You coward, you rat
You're an insect that's all a bloodthirsty gnat
This is my reward for being your mate
But I'd rather be in prison than have your fate.

One day, one day
What comes around?
Goes around!

I wrote this in Belmarsh prison thinking of the slag **Richard Leddingham or Richard Green which was his new name given to him by the law.**

Remember his name and if you ever meet him, then spit in his eye, he is the lowest form of human being there is.

School mates and growing up

School days...
My earliest memories of school were when we moved to a house in
Mossville gardens in Morden. It was mum and dad's first house and they
loved it. The house was a three bed detached house with a huge
conservatory and large back garden. It had a garage on the side which my
father made into a small gym by putting up a punch bag and a few weights.
Nearby there was a school called Hillcross primary and middle school. The
school had a massive field and it was there that i made my first mates. Just
around the corner there lived a boy called Mark Modena who had Italian
parents. I remember one time where i stayed at their house for a couple of
days and gave marks mum a nervous breakdown. Its true she actually went
to the doctors after looking after me for two days!
Another time i remember my dad coming home after the pub shut and
walking into the house with a bloody great big Great Dane dog, he had
found it wandering the streets so stopped his car and brought it home, i
could hear my mum moaning from upstairs in my room and when i heard
the dog I ran downstairs and saw this bloody great bear jumping around
everywhere.
The next morning i remember waking up to this horrible smell, I came
downstairs and opened the living room door and saw this giant puddle of
diorehia all across the floor. I called out for my mum to come downstairs
but my sister ran down and walked straight into the puddle, she slipped
over in it and was covered. I laughed my head off as she sat there covered
in shit crying and screaming.
Later that day my mum came to pick me up from school with our new dog,
the dog was dragging my poor mum all up the road.
 He was a lovely dog but we soon found out why he was wandering the
streets, he was just too uncontrollable. One day when I came home from
school he was gone, my mum and dad had had enough. A few days earlier
when my dad was out and my mum was working at Tooting Market the dog
decided to chew everything in the house. One of the neighbours saw the
dog at the front window chewing and ripping at my mum's nets and the
neighbour said it looked like a mad gorilla tearing the place apart.

Talking about dogs we had another dog a few months after, one night my sister was walking home and an Alsatian followed her home. My mum called the police who said that if anyone didn't claim the dog then we could keep it if we wanted. We named the dog 'Shane' and he was a lovely dog. I remember once when i used to open the window in the conservatory and he would jump in and out of the garden through the open window, i showed my mum and she loved what i had taught the dog to do. Later that day my dad came home and she called him into the conservatory to show him what we had taught the dog to do! Next to the window was a large pane of glass, about four feet by four feet, now my mum opened the window and called the dog who was in the back garden, i don't know why but maybe she was standing in front of the open window, she tapped the window and shouted for the dog, "c'mon Shane jump!" she said as my dad stood there wondering what was happening. next moment the dog jumped straight through the four-foot pane of glass to almighty racket, glass smashed everywhere as my dad's face became an absolute picture.
What a bloody trick that was! Teaching the poor dog to jump through a big pane of glass. Poor Shane freaked out and ran inside the house as my dad shouted out, he ran after tie dog to see if he was okay and then came running back into the conservatory where me and mum where still standing. I was laughing as he shouted at her, "what the fucking hell was that!"
"He was supposed to jump through the window." My mum said
"Oh fucking was he!" my dad said still in disbelief at what had just happened.

I had some great memories and not so great times at Mossville gardens. A lot of the time i lived there my father was in prison and my mum had to work so i had the house to myself a lot. I remember in the winters when i would come home from school around four or four thirty when it was getting dark would be around ten years of age and had my own front door key would open the front door and carefully reach inside to switch the light on in the hall, the house would be pitch black so I used to feel scared to walk in until the lights were on.
The times when my dad wasn't in prison were the most fun times. The house was always busy with his mates coming round. My dad owned his own car site in Camberwell near Peckham so there were always flash cars outside our house. Some of the cars i remember him coming home in were

A Rolls Royce, Corvette stingray, a Lamborghini, a Lamborghini–Citroen, a Jensen interceptor, e-type jags!

Another great memory I had was when my father used to have card nights round the house, he had this green felt table top which his mates would set up after a night down the pub, they would all come back around midnight and sit there drinking and playing cards till the early hours. I was in bed but i would often walk out my room and sit on the stairs watching my dad and his mates playing around.

I remember once being spotted and my dad called me down, he was teaching me boxing at the that time so he asked me to 'shape-up' for his mates, I got into my boxing pose and started to throw jabs and hooks as everyone cheered. My dad's good friend Terry Marsh was there and he gave me a pound note which made everyone else reach into their pockets and give me money. I went to bed that night with over a tenner in my pyjamas.

Some of my first mates around this time were the twins Frank and Terry Nichols, they were a couple of years older than me and had a younger brother Danny who was in my class at school. There dad was a long distance lorry driver so he wasn't at home much so the twins were always staying over at my house.

Life in those days was just one big adventure, we would often stay up all night and then around dawn get on our push bikes and ride up to Wimbledon common, we would just muck about all day long getting into different bits of bother.

One day we on the old factory estate off Durnsford road near Wandsworth, the factory estate was a mixture of old abandoned warehouses and single story offices and most of the offices had the windows smashed so it was a paradise for young mischievous boys.

There was also an old building which i used to call it a chalk mill, i don't know if it was but it was an old wooden building with an open bottom which had a mountain of old chalk like powder on the ground. On the first floor there was an old rope pulley system which was obviously used one time to lift the chalk or powder. The building was falling apart and you had to be very careful when walking on the wooden floorboards as most of them were broken or rotting. There was also a long wooden slide attached to the first floor, we had countless times tried to fix the holes in the slide but it was not steep enough or slippery enough for us to get any real speed when we slid down.

Anyway on this day we started out by the offices throwing stones at some of the windows until we made a small fire, for some reason which i don't remember we found an old lorry tyre and decided to throw it onto the fire, we then went into the offices to explore leaving the tyre on the small fire. A few minutes later we came out of the building and there was thick black smoke everywhere, it was unbelievable the amount of smoke. Frank Nichols tried to kick the tyre off the fire but the flames were too high and because of the smoke we couldn't get close enough. Then just as we were all backing away we heard someone shout at us. We turned round to see it was a policeman who was now running over to us. In those days the police used to wear the long heavy black tunics and pointed hats. The copper shouted at us again and that was all we needed to set off like greyhounds being released from the tracks. I headed straight for the chalk mill where i knew we could climb up the ladder onto the first floor and then jump down the slide. The twins followed me then so did the copper. As we were running he was constantly shouting for us to stop and blowing his whistle at us. We reached the old chalk building where immediately i flew up the ladder and then turned to help Frank and terry, the copper was now almost within grabbing distance so once we were all up the ladder we headed straight for the slide. I pushed my pals out first and then turned to see the cop had now climbed the old wooden ladder and was making his way towards us. He screamed out again and then started to run for us but what happened next would etched into my mind forever, he took three or four steps and then jumped over some old bits of wood on the floor but when he landed his foot went straight through the old rotten floorboards. He yelled out and then just froze like a man who had just wandered onto cracking ice. He looked up at us with a look of horror just before the floor gave way and he fell crashing through the floor boards right into the mountain of chalk dust below. I can remember at first feeling a bit of concern but when I saw the cloud of chalk dust rising into the air and the copper coughing and calling us every name under the sun quickly found the hilarious side of what had just happed. I looked down at him with a huge smile on my face and he was absolutely smothered in the dirty white chalk dust.

"Are you alright?" I shouted down to him.

"I will fucking kill ya, you little bastard!" he screamed back.

"Yeah, in your dreams copper!" I said back to him laughing as I looked down through the broken floor and saw him raging mad, he was coughing and completely coated in the dust. I just broke down in laughter which made him even madder. He cursed at us again and then grabbed a piece of wood which he threw at us.

"You wait till I get my fucking hands on you, you little bastards!" he screamed as we decided to run for the sewers which were across the plough road and were always a good place to hide. We ran across the busy road and turned to see the copper running after us with a cloud of dust coming off him, at the entrance to the sewers which was after a small bridge there was a small hole in the fence, we could only just squeeze through it ourselves so there was no way an adult could follow. I remember pushing my friends through the gap and then turning to see how close the copper was to us, he was just across the road and could see where we were heading so he just ran into the road with his hand outstretched to tell the cars to stop. The next moment he was hit by a car and knocked onto the bonnet, the car screeched to a halt as i pushed myself through the gap. I looked back and saw that the copper wasn't that injured, he was straight back on his feet as cars on both side of the road stopped to see if he was okay. He didn't even speak to the drivers, he just raced over to the gap in the fence and tried to put his leg through, he was absolutely seething but there was no way he could follow us now. We made our getaway and decided that we would stay away from that are for a couple of weeks, at least until the copper calmed down. I remember telling my dad what had happened that evening when he came home with Johnny Cheshire the old boxer. My dad burst into laughter and said I bet the copper got slaughtered by all the other coppers when he went back to the station smothered in dust!

In those days when i was around ten they were glorious days, no worries or stress, life just seemed one big adventure. I used to go out often with my father; sometimes he would take me over the car site with him where i would see my Uncles' Ted and Den. I always loved the site as i would try to sit in all the cars.

The car site was only a couple of miles away from the old Kent road and the famous pub the Thomas a Becket. We would go to the pub often where they had a gym upstairs.

Alan minter the world middleweight champion was good friends with my father and we would go to watch him train where my dad would often see his very good friend Alex Steene I remember one day when we heading up to the car site and we were driving through Tooting high street, suddenly my dad just pulled the car over to the kerb and jumped out his seat, he shouted out to a fella walking down the road.

"OI!" my dad shouted at the man who turned to see it was my father and then scarpered up the road followed by my dad. Suddenly a black guy jumped into our car and started to follow my dad who was now running after the man shouting at him to stop. The black guy was a pal of my dad's and had just on the off chance seen what was happening so ran over the road to help. We drove up the road until we found my dad who had unfortunately lost the fella who had jumped on the back of a bus and got away. My dad saw his friend driving and said hello and thanked him. We didn't say much about what had happened as things like this were always happening anyway but in later years i found out that the man my dad was chasing was Johnny Bindon the famous actor / tough guy. Bindon and my father ended up good pals again after this. I did hear a story later on that my dad found Bindon one day at Max's place in Garret Lane, Bindon had a tough guy reputation at the time and my dad was told by someone that he was saying something bad about my father. My dad anyway confronted him in Maxes and John said he said no such thing, after that they became good pals till the day John died.

Another good memory I had was when my dad took me to the Thomas a Becket gym one afternoon when the world champion sugar ray Leonard was attending, the place was absolutely mobbed out and you couldn't get near the door. My dad then saw Joey Cannon a well-known south east London face who was working the door. A few moments later Joey got me and my dad inside where I got my picture done with the champ.

All in all, I had a very memorable childhood, there were hard times but fucking hell I did have some fun.

When trouble came knocking!

My early memories of Mossville gardens and my first years of Hillcross were not always fun and joy. There were some very hard times as well.
Around the age of ten I had what I can remember my first encounter with the police and saw just how much they actually hated my family.
One morning when i was getting up for school i had just came downstairs when the front door came crashing in and what seemed to me an army of uniformed policeman came storming into the house. What i can remember is all the shouting and my mother quickly grabbing me, we were forced into the living room and told to wait as they went upstairs to get my father out of bed. For the next couple of hours, the coppers turned our house upside down as they searched everywhere, they even pulled up the carpet in the living room and pulled up some floor boards. Me and my mum and dad were made to sit in the front room under a guard of at least ten coppers as we could hear them stampeding through the house like a heard of fucking elephants. I can remember my dad being angry and then after they searched his car outside they came back into the front room and arrested him and my mother.
My father was arrested for firearms which they said they found in his car but which was later found out in court was planted by the crooked copper Harold Hannigan.
At such an early age I was shown first hand just how bent some of the old bill really were, they took my mum and dad away and left me in tears with a neighbour not knowing what had just happened. My mum was released a few hours later but they remanded my father to Brixton prison.
A few months later when the case came to trial it was thrown out by the judge who said it was a complete farce, nevertheless they held my dad in prison for a few months which turned me and my mum's lives upside down and what was more they had made an impression on me which would forever make me look at the old bill as a corrupt and vindictive bunch of arseholes.
I used to go up to visit my father in Brixton with my mum and in those days you used to be able to take food into the prisons when they were on remand. I remember my mum making a roast dinner and covering it with tin foil and we would jump in her car and drive the short distance to the prison where we would queue up until we were allowed in.

One day I was visiting with my mum and as all young boys think I did something where I didn't think of the consequences. While my mum was getting ready I was in my room and I used to have a toy gun and holster, it was a present at one Christmas which came with a cowboy hat and sheriff's badge. Anyway I hid the gun in my clothing and we went to the prison to see my father.

We got through the first door okay but then when we got to the security I was suddenly pulled away and searched, the screws found the toy gun which didn't take them a second glance to see exactly what it was but then after they had a quick chat amongst themselves they hit the alarm and arrested both me and my mum. The whole prison was thrown into lock down and all the visits cancelled. Me and my mum were taken away to a room where I can only assume one of the prison governors came to see what was happening. My mum went absolutely ballistic at me and shortly after a couple of police arrived. I was taken away where the police kept on asking me if my mum knew about the gun, she didn't so I told them she never knew, I was asked why I had it and I said I got it as a present and wanted to show it to my dad, they kept on and on asking if my dad asked me to sneak it in and I kept on telling them that he never knew about it or my mum.

We were held all day at the prison and finally released where my mum dragged me to the car and told me I was going straight to bed when we got home. It was unbelievable really but I suppose prisons have their rules and regulations and looking back at it my mum was lucky not to be arrested. My dad was also given a hard time, not just by the screws but by the other cons who all had their visits cancelled for the day, let's just say my dad was not the most popular man on the wing that day!

When my dad was found not guilty and returned home things quickly returned back to normal. I was getting to that mischievous age and although my dad had just lost six months of his freedom I had just been given six months of extra freedom which definitely had an effect on me. During the time my dad was in prison my mum was working in tooting market everyday so when I finished school I would come home to an empty house. I quickly learnt how to cook for myself and how to basically look after myself.

Some days i would come home from school and go to Morden where i would jump on the tube train and go to tooting where I would wait for my mum to finish at 5;30 and another day I would just get on my push bike and explore everywhere I could.

Around this time, I was hanging around with two brothers who lived nearby Michael (Mike) and Steven Cordingley. Mike was the biggest boy in my school, eleven years old and almost six-foot-tall so together we used to get into all kinds of bother.

One of the things we used to love to do was after school get the tube to the elephant and castle leisure centre as in those days the leisure centre had a swimming pool and it was one of the first swimming pools in the country to have a new thing called a wave machine. We would go there as often as we could as it was great fun, an alarm would go off every fifteen minutes or so and then the whole pool would be transformed into these massive waves swirling you around, we would play for hours until it closed and then get the tube back home to Morden.

My mum would struggle with me when my father was away, it wasn't her fault it was just me growing up and wanting to discover the world. I was constantly now getting in trouble at school around this time with fights and attitude problems.

One time my mother was called to school because the head master wanted to speak with her about the school 'pen pal' exchange. When a French boy would come and stay at our house for a week and then i would go to France and stay with his parents.

Everything was booked for a boy called Paul to come over but then a week before my mum was asked to come in because of 'Certain fears' as the school pronounced it. Basically they were not keen to have him stay at my house because of my father's reputation and problems with the law. My mum kicked up a huge fuss and said it would not be fair on me, after a few days the school relented and Paul was allowed to come over and stay at my house. In hindsight he should have stayed in France as we didn't get on at all. I think it was barely a day until I punched him in the mouth, my dad went mad at me and gave me a right clump and then took us both out to the wimpy in Morden. But the damage was done and after that me and Paul never liked each other, that was a silly mistake from me as i had yet to go to France to stay with Paul and his two brothers, there was a small sea and a few hundred miles for him to get his own back. When i did go to France it was a disaster, Paul and me fought each other on the first day, the second day i had a fight with his elder brother, the third day his mother broke down in tears because I didn't like any of the French grub she was cooking and the fourth day I decided to run away and got arrested by the police trying to

bunk onto a train. The rest of week I spent staying with one of the teachers which was better than the piss hole I was staying. One of my memories was watching Paul's father digging some flower beds in the back garden one day and after a few hours with the shovel he was sitting in their front room with all the family around him making an almighty fuss because he had a few blisters on his hands, his wife had a bowl of water and was washing him as he flinched in pain while his three sons sat around him all looking worried like he had been shot or something. I remember vividly smirking and thinking what a fucking wanker, that was the night I decided to make my escape, i just couldn't bear to be around these people anymore.
 A pal of mine Mark Brane meanwhile was having the time of his life, his pen-pal lived on a farm and mark told me they would play games kicking the pigs and sticking flick knives through the rolls of cheese, it sounded like a right adventure while I was stuck with my bunch of idiots.

Another thing around this time I remember is when mike and Steve Cordingley's parents decided to ban their children from hanging around with me anymore because of my father. They said we were gangsters or some cobblers and they wouldn't have their kids round our house. This went on for a few months with me not being allowed into mikes house or even knock on his door, but we just met up the road and after a while when they saw that mike was taking no notice i slowly started to be allowed into the house again. This story however has a real irony attached to it, years later my dad started working with a man we called Irish nick who had his own small double glazing business, my dad ended up buying half the business and guess who worked for Irish nick??? Yep Mike Cordingleys father! The same father who didn't want his son hanging around with a gangster's son who was now himself working for a gangster! .... Funny how money can make people jump from their moral high horse!

Another horrible time was just a couple of months after my dad was released from prison and his best friend Terry Marsh was killed by another friend of my father, a man called mad Ronnie Fryer.
Terry was a lovely man, he wasn't what you would call a crook like some of my dad's mates, he wasn't like Johnny Nash or Roy Shaw or the twins but he was just as loyal, he was always with my dad and was for a time like a second father to me. My mum thought the world of Terry and his wife June. In those days my dad had three very close local friends, Terry Marsh, Peter Brayham and Alec Steene, my dad still had some very good friends, men like

Peter Marshal, Peter Tilley, Roy Shaw and Johnny Nash and his brothers but Terry, Peter and Alec all lived local to us and there was hardly a day that went by when I never saw at least one of them round our house.

I remember being devastated when I came home from school and found my mum crying. I got on my push bike and went round Terry's house in St Helier's avenue to see his son Nicky who was only a couple of years older than me and we were good pals. Nicky was home with his two elder brothers Ray and Terry Jnr and all three of them were in shock. I stayed with them until my mum came round to pick me up.

My father was abroad where he went to Monte Carlo to see Carlos Monzon fight but as soon as he heard the news he got the first plane home.

Dad was absolutely livid and he put the word out he was looking for Mad Ronnie.

Mad Ronnie went into hiding as he everyone including the old bill was looking for him. A few days later he walked into Wimbledon police station completely guilt ridden and gave himself up.

Ronnie fryer was arrested for murder and then got remanded in Brixton prison, what happened next is up for debate but he ended up dying in prison from cyanide.

Over the years there have been many different theories of what happened to Ronnie, I have my own view but I guess the real story went to the grave with my father and Ronnie.

Prison

In my life I have worked with many different people and most of them stories will go with me to my grave.

since I was young, I always had a sixth sense to remain 'one step ahead' so to say. I lived on the edge for many years but I was fortunate enough or clever enough to remain a free man.

When the long arm of the law finally grabbed my collar, it was ironically for something I never did!

Now I hear many people saying, 'you got away with this and that' so things just caught up with you.

'BOLLOCKS!' I say to that!

Imagine this then if you believe that, let's say every night you speed home from work and break the speed limit but every night you get away with it, then one night you drive home doing thirty all the way and a copper pulls you over for speeding. You ask what's wrong and he says 'speeding' but you reply I have done thirty all the way home. Then the copper replies, yes tonight you did but last night I think you were speeding, so I'm nicking you for it tonight!

let's be honest what would you all say?

I would say ' BOLLOCKS!'

Anyway back to the early nineties and my time in prison.

Believe it or not I was arrested by the regional crime squad for information that linked me with the proceeds of the Brinks Mat robbery…. It's a long story but complete cobblers, typical old bill stuff making up fairy tales.

Anyway on this day I had 'NINE' unmarked police cars following me to a meeting. I arrived and met someone who was working for my father who at this time was in prison. This man was a straight business man and was weekly giving my mother some money which was my father's share of the business. I say straight but he like most of us had a few rough edges. He knew at the time I was working with people in South Africa, so on the

meeting he asked me if they would be interested in counterfeit currency?
I said maybe they will and with that he gave me an envelope with £500 of
the dodgy notes. A few minutes later the window went through on the car
and I was dragged out by three armed police, the next thing cars appeared
from everywhere and I was cuffed and thrown on the ground, they
searched my friend's car for what I later found out was an anonymous 'tip-
off' looking for 50KG of cannabis resin. (proceeds of the Brinks matt robbery
– I honestly don't know where the coppers get this crap from!)
Anyway, they found nothing except for the envelope of counterfeit notes
which was still on the dashboard.
When they found the dosh I was cuffed lying face down on the ground with
some big fucker kneeling on my back and a gun pointed in my ear.
Now remember the man with me was my father's business partner in a legit
business company and was giving my mum money every week while dad
was away, this guy had a financial advisors license or whatever they call it
so I knew if he was caught with dodgy money then his business was over
and so would the 'bung' to my mum every week.
Biting my fucking lip and going against everything I have ever believed in I
shouted out that the envelope was mine, before the coppers started asking
him why he had that in his car.
To be honest it made me feel fucking sick, I had NEVER made a statement or
owned up to anything but this time it involved family so I took the blame.
 A few months later I was convicted and sent to prison..
So here I was doing porridge for something I never done, I didn't know the
fella was turning up to the meeting with an envelope of dodgy notes, I went
to see him about a legit PLC company which we were looking at taking over.
So now I'm in Brixton prison, walking out my cell in the morning to the voice
of some poxy screw shouting at me to ' DO YOUR FUCKING COLLAR UP!'
Prison to me, really didn't bother me, I was more pissed off to the fact that
the old bill had one over on me. I did my time the right way, didn't make no
waves and kept myself to myself. I had a couple of rows but then that's
what happens when you get thrown into an environment with hundreds of
mainly mugs who think they're tough!
I did hate Brixton though, it had a stench about it that was in your clothes,

in the food, in bloody everything. I was there for about seven days when one night the cell door was opened at around nine at night. Two screws called me and then said I had a phone call.

"What do you mean a fucking phone call? I asked looking as surprised as them.

"Downstairs, it's your old man on the phone." One of them replied looking proper pissed off.

So they led me downstairs where I walked into their office and picked up the phone to speak to my father who was on remand in the unit double Cat A in Belmarsh.

"Joey, you alright son?"

"Yes dad, what's the matter?" I answered worried.

"Nothing, we're all here having a protest, we ain't going back to our cells unless I get their word they will bring you over here." My dad answered clearly angered.

"Now, do what you got to do and we're do what we have to do!" he added.

So two days later I was transported to the top security prison in the UK, all courtesy of my father and his mates and three IRA men who refused to get locked up unless I was moved.

At first I was pleased to out of the 'shithole' Brixton, and being in Belmarsh meant I could visit my father on Saturday mornings.

When I arrived at Belmarsh and taken to the house block I was given straight away a single cell, which is pretty unusual, I was two cells away from an old family friend Ronnie Fields who was arrested with Charlie Kray. I've known Ronnie for years so I was given loads of snout, yorkie bars and few boxes or Ritz crackers.

I found Belmarsh much easier than Brixton, it was cleaner and the food was a hundred times better, the only downside was I was now in a top security prison when I was a cat D prisoner, I would have gone to Ford open prison but because of my dad and his mates, that wasn't going to happen now! Anyway when I was released in 1993 I can proudly say I have never been back.

Since then I have been a president of a union, a company director of two PLC companies. A manager of music acts such as Mark Morrison and Brian Harvey, a film producer, an actor and a boxing promoter and manager and now an author.

If anyone can claim to be 'reformed' then surely I could wear that tag!

I have also in the past, joined community programs, giving speeches to young people on staying 'out of the nick'

I am not proud of my times in prison but neither am I ashamed, I have no regrets, no remorse and if I am honest it was all part of becoming the man I am.

There is an irony to this short tale, whilst I was away the man I was protecting moved house and left the country … thus stopped paying my mum her money. But I did the right thing, I can hold my head up high!

Me and Dad in Kenya, a few years later after this picture was taken we would share the same Prison.

South Africa and Lady Janet and locked up in Angola

What is it with the aristocracy and so called villains? Maybe they like our charm and our cheeky care free attitude. Whatever it is I have met a few of them over the years and another thing they love is getting their hands dirty and doing what they call a naughty piece of business. One such lady was Lady Janet, I won't tell you her real name but she was a distant cousin to the queen and her grandfather was very publically killed by the IRA!

I first met Janet through my father when he was introduced to her at our film office at Pinewood studios. My father and Jan as we called her got on really well. She was in her late fifties but had a wicked sense of humour. She spoke with an impeccable English accent but loved to mix with the lads!

anyway ... my father was in prison and lady Jan had flown back to Pretoria south Africa to set up a business with her sister in Johannesburg. One morning I woke up to answer the phone where it was Jan, she asked me to write down a number and quickly go to a call box and call her back. I threw a tracksuit on and drove to a call box and called the number.

"joey, I need you to come to south Africa." She said straight away.

"Jan, I can't I have things to do here."

"it's very important, this could be the big one darling."

"what do you mean?"

"I have a warehouse in Boksberg, it is in Johannesburg, we are setting up a massive LF (Long-Firm fraud)." She replied.

"Jan I would love to but I just can't get out at the moment."

"joey, I need you to run it, we will be partners and we can earn fortunes." She replied.

I remember pausing for a moment as the word fortunes went through my mind. I told her I would call her back later and see what I could do.

All what was left of the day and the next I couldn't get the thought of South Africa out of my mind. Things were getting very heated in the UK for me, my father was on remand in Belmarsh for what they were calling the largest conspiracy ever in the UK to smuggle drugs and my pals had just been arrested for smuggling fifty kilos of hash from Spain.

I could feel the noose tightening around my neck, the law was nicking everyone and I must be on their radar somewhere.

When I told my mum I was thinking of going away she wasn't too happy, especially after my last trip abroad which saw me gaoled in Spain and I was also picking up a few pensions every week for her as my father wasn't able to do it himself.

The next day I called a travel agent and found out the price of a flight, it was around £600 and I was skint at the time, all I had was my car which was a 2.9 Ford Granada ghia. I made a few calls and was offered £3000 for it so after an hour or so thinking about everything I went down and sold it.

That was it now; I had no car so I was now committed to going to Africa.

A few days later I was on a brand new South African airlines jumbo jet and on my way to Johannesburg. I was really excited as I loved to travel and I had always wanted to go to Africa. I was heading into the unknown and that was a place I loved to go.

When I arrived in Johannesburg I was picked up by Lady Janet and we drove to her relative's house in Pretoria, we spoke on the way about the warehouse and long firm and I was feeling really excited about getting to work.

When we arrived at her relatives house I was introduced to her family and introduced to my new living quarters... a caravan parked in the bloody drive!

I was also introduced to her nephew Mike who was the same age as me and had just come out of national service and was gun crazy, I couldn't believe it when I went into his room and it was full of handguns rifles and semi-automatics. We spent the next hour in the garden shooting things which seemed as normal to him as me back home making a bbq in my garden. I couldn't believe as this was the first day and I'm shooting pump shotguns at the trees and firing sniper rifles across the field, it was bloody fantastic.

Later that night Mike asked me to join him to go out for a few drinks, Pretoria was crazy! I remember driving with him on the way to a bar and seeing caravans at the side of the road where AWB soldiers were standing outside signing people up, they looked like Nazis and Mike told me they were nutters, real Afrikaners, mike had English roots so he wants so hard line as the Dutch or Afrikaans south Africans.

That night I forget or didn't realise we were something like 5000 ft above sea level, I never knew anything about altitude but after a few beers and vodkas I was bloody pissed. We ended up coming back around one after a right laugh and I went straight to bed in my caravan. As soon as I got into the bed my fucking head was spinning so I opened the window quickly and was sick all down the side.

The next morning, I woke up and walked outside and to my horror I saw all the sick stuck down the side of the white caravan, my head was killing me but I felt so embarrassed I found an old cloth and wiped it off.

Great start to the day!

I had some breakfast and then me and Jan left for the warehouse in Boksberg on the outskirts of Johannesburg, about 40 miles. On the way Jan was telling me all about the long firm and how we were going to earn fortunes.

After about an hour we arrived at the warehouse and I walked into this bloody great empty warehouse! All that was in there at the far end was a pallet of cheap shoes. I walked over looking and feeling a bit pissed off.

"is this it?" I asked hoping that there was more somewhere.

Before Jan answered I saw a small man walk out from an office, he looked like a rough version of Leo sayer I remember thinking, Jan introduced me to him where I found out he was originally from Liverpool and had been living out there for a year or so.

"this is Paul," Jan said as I held out my hand

"where's all the other stuff?" I asked him without saying hello.

"we have to get the bank account set up first." He replied not having a clue with the bombshell he had just hit me with.

"what do you mean, bank account? Haven't you got that sorted out already?" I asked him before turning to Jan.

"whose name is the company going in?" I added raising my voice to lady Jan.

"don't worry about that Joe we will sort that out" she answered back showing how fucking naïve she was.

"sort that out! You told me everything was set up already, how the fuck can I run a long firm with no bank account?"

To say I was disappointed was a big big fucking understatement! I was thousands of miles away from home with hardly any money and standing in a great big empty fucking warehouse with nothing to do other than do everything myself to get this up and running.
"what front money do we have?" I then asked Jan, who looked back at me with a look on her face that told me she never had a clue what I was talking about.
"money?" she asked looking embarrassed.
"yes Jan, money to start the bank account and money to use when opening up lines of credit with companies, with no bank account we will have to pay for a few orders and then gradually build up some kind of relationships, no one is just going to start giving us loads of stuff on credit."

Surprise surprise lady Jan the member of the aristocracy was skint!
So with sod all to do at the warehouse and as we were close to Johannesburg, Jan decided to take me to meet one of her friends who I will call Sarah who was also known as the diamond queen of south Africa.
Sarah was a very rich lady of Johannesburg and lived in a big house near Sandhurst, a rich suburb of the city, she was married to a Jewish guy named Shai who I soon discovered was very successful member of the Johannesburg underworld.
We had some lunch and then got talking about a few things where I was then introduced to Shai's nephew, a kid named Dion who was another kid my age and had just like mike not long come out of national service.
Me and Dion clicked straight away and he invited me out with him that night where he told Jan I could stay with him at his house in Blairgowie which was another suburb of Jo'Burg.
That night we went out and had a right laugh, Dion was mad as a hatter, we got drunk, pulled a couple of girls and ended back at his house with the girls around 3 in the morning.

The next morning, we woke up and had something to eat which he got his maid to cook us and then we drove to Sarah and Shai's home in Sandhurst but as we pulled up we found the front of the house had been sprayed with bullets. Dion buzzed the gates and we were quickly let into the house by Moses who was the gardener / handyman of the house.

We walked inside and Shai was sitting with a few guys who all had guns and I spotted straight away that this didn't look good, they were talking in Afrikaans so I didn't have a fucking clue what was going on but I knew it was about the bullet holes in the side of the house.

Suddenly Dion walked over and handed me a pump shotgun.

"you know how to use this?" he said as he pushed it into my arms.

"yeah course I do." I answered trying to sound strong as I didn't want them to see me look weak.

"Good! you stay here and guard the house, make sure no one gets in, we are going somewhere." Dion then said which made me think … what the fuck have got myself into here.

So they all run out getting into three cars leaving me standing on my own with a gun in my hand minding a house for someone I had only just met a few days earlier.

This was the start of things which got very crazy, very fast.

I ended up moving in with Dion as the warehouse thing was a complete waste of time and Dion was doing a few errands for Shai where I went with him and picked up some rands, it wasn't a fortune but I was having a good time. Shai was also getting to trust me and he was handing me a few jobs as well which were mainly driving jobs…. Shai was an intriguing character, he wasn't tough to look at but he was very tough inside and completely fearless.

Over the next week or so he began to ask me more and more to go with him on errands, I was given a handgun which I carried in my trousers everywhere we went and I suppose I was becoming a bit of a minder to Shai who introduced me to everyone we met as his English partner and also a friend of Charlie Richardson who was a bit of a legend over there. Charlie spent some time in south Africa and got up to some naughty things, me being Charlie's pal kept me in good stead.

I also discovered that Shai was in the middle of a gang war with a competitor over some business deals and that he was into many things and he was deeply involved with ANC and Winnie Mandela.

One time he took me to this big house just on the outskirts of Soweto, it was like tony Montana's house in Scarface and there were armed security officers all over the place holding AK47's.

The house belonged to Andrew Pinaar, who was very high up in the ANC but let's just say he didn't act or speak like a politician, nor live like one, he was very well respected and very feared.

I got on well with Andrew and before long he started to ask me to go with him on a few jobs, we would regularly go to the bank in Soweto, where I would watch his back even though he never needed it. He would walk straight into the bank and straight into the bank manager's office, Andrew never had to wait on line, in fact I never saw him once wait for anything.

One day he took me to meet Winnie Mandela in Soweto where they spoke about a few ANC things before disappearing into another room where they needed to speak about some things without anyone hearing.

As I was waiting in Mandela's house, Shai and Dion arrived, Dion sat next to me and Shai knocked on the door where Winnie and Andrew were talking, Shai walked into the room and after a short while they all came out, we all said goodbye to Winnie and then drove back to Andrews home.

When we got there Shai and Dion spoke in Afrikaans and then Dion turned to me.

"you want to come to Angola?" he asked me

"where the fucks Angola?" I replied not having a clue if he was talking about a place or somewhere to eat.

"it's up north, three days' drive, we can earn good money."

"yeah, why not!" I said thinking about the words good money.

"you take three jeeps, two you leave there and then all come back in one." Shai said sitting down next to me.

So that was that, I was now going to go to Angola, a country in the middle of a civil war and dangerous as fuck. The deal was simple if it worked, we were driving two stolen top of range jeeps and meeting up with the rebels where they would give us a bag of rough cut diamonds in exchange for the jeeps, we would then bring the rough cut diamonds back to Shai in Johannesburg where he would have them cut and then sold.

My share of the money was around £2000 which for a week's work in those days was good money. I did feel hesitant but I was involved now, I was working with these people and to pull out would make me look like a fucking mug or someone with no heart.

The time was set for us to leave in three days so that night me and Dion went down the local pub in Blairgowie for a few drinks and to see if there were any girls about. Just a nice night out? Yeah right this was south Africa, a country like the fucking wild west.

In south Africa everyone has guns in their home and everyone carries them about, in fact if you leave your house and leave your gun at home and someone breaks in and uses your guns in a killing then you can pretty much be assured that you will be nicked for murder so everyone carries their guns with them.

Walking in the pub is crazy, you walk in carrying a pump shotgun and just hand it to the barman to hold like it's the most normal thing in the world. Anyway this night me and Dion are throwing back the beers until closing time, we grab the guns from behind the bar and walk out, remember I'm pissed, holding car keys, got a 38 pistol in my shorts and a pump shotgun in my other hand. I walk straight out and walk straight into two cops. I almost fucking feinted! I'm pissed, driving and got two guns on me! In London id be sitting in the cell for at least fifteen years but this was south Africa.

I was just about to run when Dion spoke to the cops.

"everything okay?"

"Yarr, we just have some problems with the kaffers." Answered one of the cops.

"Do you need some help?" replied Dion showing the cop his rifle.

"no its okay boys, just drive home safely, the animals are restless tonight!" replied the copper.

I was fucking stunned, I actually started to laugh at the crazy comparison with living here to living in London. It was crazy but I was starting to love it. On the way home I stopped at a red light

"DRIVE!" Dion shouted next to me

"it's a fucking red light!" I shouted back

Dion leaned over me pulled his gun out and through my window shot the fucking red light, my ears went deaf with loud ringing as Dion started to laugh,

"it's not red no more." He said though I could barely hear him.

So, so far the day had been quite adventurous but it was nothing to what happened when we got back to Dion's house.

We had been in the house for about an hour when all of sudden Dion said what's that as he heard a noise, he turned down the volume on the tv and we both listened to see what we could hear.

"get the guns!" Dion then said looking concerned.

I jumped up and was joined by Dion who grabbed the pump action shotgun and I picked up the pistol on the table and we both sneaked up to the windows and peaked out by the curtains.

"someone is out there" Dion then said as he moved towards the door.

"get the door." He then added as I walked over.

The outside to Dion's house had a big veranda which was covered in that corrugated see through plastic sheets, you know the curved stuff they put on garage roofs.

I grabbed the handle and opened the door and Dion hesitantly poked his head out and then suddenly shouted and let two shots go into the plastic roof, there was a loud scream and then someone fell, Dion let another shot go and the person on the roof staggered across the roof and then fell into the next door neighbours garden where a dog started to attack him. Suddenly all the flood lights came on in the neighbour's garden and someone came out, Dion jumped on the wall and was pointing his gun at the injured man now being attacked by the dog.

"YOU FUCKING PIECE OF SHIT!" Dion shouted as he then started to speak with the neighbour who had come out with his gun and was calling the dog off.

"JOE CALL THE COPS!" Dion then shouted to me.

I was in shock, Dion had just shot some poor black fella and was telling me to call the cops, yeah right! I thought, I'm fucking out of here went through my head, I ran into the house and grabbed my suitcase and was throwing my clothes into it as quick as I could when Dion walked in

"What are doing?"

"you just fucking shot someone! I'm fucking off!"

"why." Dion asked looking shocked.

"Why??? You just filled some poor cunt with buckshot, we need to fuck off mate!" I said back to frantically.

"Stop!" Dion said calmly as he walked over and grabbed my bag, "It's okay, the cops will take him away, we will not be trouble." He added.

As Dion finished talking a siren was heard outside the house but it wasn't the cops it was armed security as nearly all the houses had armed security on call with panic buttons, suddenly the whole street was live as two more cars pulled up followed by a three police cars. I was fucked now, I couldn't even get away even if I wanted to so I walked outside and just followed Dion as the security grabbed the injured man and took him over to the police.

Next thing a cop walks over and asks Dion what happened and Dion starts telling him what happened and that the man was a burglar, another cop came over to me holding a small board where he was writing his report.

"what happened?" he asked me looking up at the roof and noticing the holes from the shotgun

"I don't know; I was inside in bed I didn't see anything. "I answered

"you not from here?" he asked

"nah, I'm from Australia." I said though I don't know why as I bit my lip as soon as I said it thinking I'm fucked if he asks to see my passport.

"Okay." He just sighed and again once again started to look at the roof.

"it's a shame." He then said without looking at me

"what is a shame?" I asked

"it is a shame you had to ruin such a nice roof to shoot the kaffer bastard!"

This was South Africa and to say culture shock, was a massive understatement. It was crazy we are running around with guns shooting people doing whatever we like and no one gives a fuck.

If this was London I would've been in the back of a police car on the way to the nick, looking at being banged up for a very very long time.

South Africa was off the charts, it was the wild West but I was starting to love this place, Africa to me was starting to feel like home

Me in Dion's house with one of the pump shotguns

The Journey – Botswana/ Namibia

When the day arrived to leave Jo'Burg I was looking forward to the journey, I was a bit nervous of what to expect as I knew we was going into a war zone but I felt excited, it was an adventure.
Little would I know that the name 'Angola' which sounded so exciting would live with me every day for the rest of my life.

On the morning we left, me and Dion drove to meet Shai in the middle of Johannesburg, a place called Hillbrow, which was a rough part of town and a place I had been to a few times and always had my wits about me when there or even driving through as car jacking's were very common.
We parked outside a large warehouse where Shai was standing outside talking to someone, we got out and Dion said hello to the stranger (Brian) who a later found out was coming with us. we then all walked in to the warehouse which was a mechanic car garage.
Shai led us over to two jeeps, both brand new Mercedes.
"you like." Shai said smiling to me.
"lovely." I replied

The two jeeps were both stolen but had had some work done to them, these were the cars we would drive to Angola where we would meet some chiefs out there and swap them for rough cut diamonds.
Angola was in the midst of a terrible civil war and the country was devastated, there was no economy, so the local war lords who were 'diamond rich' had nowhere to spend their money. There were no McDonalds or shopping areas, nothing, just the war!

Shai gave Dion two letters, one was full of cash and the other letter I found out later was from the ANC to give to the Angola border control which would give us safe entry into the war torn country. I cannot say for sure as it would be libellous but the letter may have been signed by Winnie Mandella?

A couple of hours later were on the road, Dion in the lead driving one of the jeeps and me behind him driving the other and Brian following me in a jeep Cherokee.

the drive would take us around two to three days depending on if we rested, it was around 1500 miles to the border of Angola (Oshiknago) and then we would drive north to a place called Savate in Angola where we would make the exchange.

We headed west to the Botswana border and entered the country, the drive itself was not too difficult as we drove on long straight roads through the middle of the bush, we were in the middle of wilderness though with absolutely nothing for miles and miles except savannah and a landscape full of wild animals.

When we crossed into Botswana, Dion stocked up on some drinks at the petrol garage where we filled the cars back up and after a short break we hit the road again.

I remember we drove nonstop into the night until around midnight where Dion started to slow down in front of me, he drove slow for a few miles until he stopped and then leant out the window and shouted for me to follow him, we then drove a few yards off the road and parked up next to some trees.

"we sleep here, get some rest!" Dion said as he walked over to my window.

"sleep where? we're in the middle of fucking nowhere!" I answered looking out into the pitch black.

"we sleep in the jeeps!" Dion replied.

An hour later we were sitting around a fire having a beer as Dion and Brian cooked some steaks over the fire, I was feeling a bit on edge as we were deep in the bush and the noises coming from the night were making me look in all directions... the night sky however was absolutely stunning as the stars shone in the night sky, there terrain was completely flat in all directions and pitch black so the stars could be seen in all their glory in all directions.

I remember after a couple of cans of beer starting to relax and then I got up and started walk off to have a piss only for Dion to call me back.

"don't go too far Joe."

"I need a piss!"

"stay near the fire, do you hear that?" Dion replied "its hyenas." He added.

Fucking hyenas, I thought… I didn't go too far as I could now hear their distinct noise they make and could tell they were getting closer as they could smell the food we were cooking. Dion then called me again and told me to come back to the fire and he then threw a log into the bush and clapped his hands loudly.

That night we all slept in our jeeps and it was an uncomfortable night's sleep as it was still hot and humid.

Daybreak was beautiful though, the sun rose gloriously across the horizon and there wasn't a cloud in the sky.

Dion and Brian started another fire and we heated some water to make some coffee, once we drank the coffee, we filled the jeeps with some fuel we had in jerry cans in the back of our vehicles and then we hit the road again.

We drove nonstop through very dry and arid land and I could feel the heat coming through the window screen, we were only a hundred or so miles from the Kalahari Desert so the air was very dry and I could feel the dust in the air.

After a few hours we stopped in a small town, where we once again filled the jeeps with petrol and filled the jerry cans, we also filled up with water and then found somewhere to wash and to have something to eat. It was a strange little shop in the middle of nowhere which had everything, rooms to rent, food a restaurant and even a small mechanics shop at the back. It was run by a Rhodesian couple who seemed very friendly and helpful.

Dion told me that we would drive the rest of the way to the Angolan border where we would sleep the night in Botswana before crossing into Angola. He said he didn't want to be travelling through Angola at night so we would cross the border first thing in the morning.

We travelled the rest of day and arrived at the border early evening where we found a small lodging house to stay. We showered and then met up downstairs in the bar.

Oshiknago (Namibia) was small but very busy town, you could just sense the skulduggery in the place, situated on the border with Angola, a country in the midst of a brutal civil war and you just sensed that this town was the hub of loads of illegal activity coming over the border.

What also surprised me the town was full of white south Africans and also white Rhodesians or Zimbabweans.

We met two men in the bar both in their forties who were former Rhodesian SAS or 'Selous scouts' as they were known. The Selous scouts were legendary figures in south Africa, I had heard of them before as one of Lady Jan's relatives was once in the corp. Jan had told me that even the British SAS held them in reverence.

Below is a brief description of them.

Created under the command of Lieutenant Colonel Ron Reid-Daly, it was organized as a mixed-race unit, consisting of recruits of both African and European descent, and whose primary mission was operating deep in insurgent-controlled territory and waging war on the hostiles' rear through irregular warfare including the use of pseudo-terrorism as a means of infiltrating the enemy. This concept of unit was very similar to the Portuguese Flechas, operating in the nearby territories of Angola and Mozambique since the late 1960s. The Selous Scouts had many black Rhodesians in their ranks who were from 50–80% of its ranks, including the first African commissioned officers in the Rhodesian Army.

The Selous Scouts acted as a combat reconnaissance force, with the mission of infiltrating Rhodesia's tribal population and guerrilla networks, pinpointing rebel groups and relaying vital information back to the conventional forces earmarked to carry out the actual attacks. Members of the regiment were trained to operate in small under-cover, clandestine teams capable of working independently in the bush for periods of weeks and of passing themselves off as rebels. The Selous Scouts were an entirely volunteer force. On one occasion, 14 out of 126 candidates—less than 12 percent of the total applicant pool—passed the selection process.

The Selous Scouts employed asymmetric warfare against their enemy, actions that ranged from the bombing of private houses, abductions, M18 Claymore mine attacks against military targets, sabotage of bridges and railways (including steam engines), assassinations, intimidation, blackmail and extortion, to the use of car bombs in the attempted assassination of Joshua Nkomo.

That night we had a few beers and some steaks and with the two former soldiers, they were great fun to be with and had an aura of danger about them, both had the trademark beard of the Selous.

I suspected they were working as mercenaries, either working with the Unita or FNLA against the communist Cuban / Russian backed MPLA. At the time I knew nothing about the Angola war but as time went on I found out everything about this brutal country.

I can also remember Dion talking to the Selous about a time when the South African army were fighting in Angola and Zaire, I remember Dion saying his uncle fought there against the commies. (as he explained it)

When we decided to go to bed we exchanged phone numbers with the men and said we would meet up soon for a beer when the men came to Jo'Burg.

I remember going up to my room that night with a smile on my face, I walked into my small room which didn't even have a ceiling light, just a small bedside lamp and a view to the street below where people were drinking and shouting.

"where the fuck am I?" I said to myself thinking about my pals back home who were probably down the pub or fucking about smoking shit round someone's house. I was in the darkest corner of Africa, a few miles from a country ravaged in war, a country I was going to enter the next morning.

This is crazy1 I thought to myself.... 2what the fuck am I doing?" I mouthed as I laid down on the spring bed.

CRAZY! .....

That night I said crazy, little did I know I was about to find out just how crazy this world can be.

ANGOLA

That morning when I woke. The first thing that came into my head was the words, "this is it!"

So far the journey had been an adventure, a bit of a laugh but now it was serious, we were going into the unknown and a place where anything could happen.

I met Dion downstairs where he asked for my passport, we were not taking them into Angola, we were taking nothing except the jeeps and some cash (Dollars)

We met Brian outside where he was fixing small flags (ANC and Red Cross) to the jeeps and after a quick cup of coffee we hit the road. The border was only a hundred yards away and when we got there, Dion stopped and walked over to the armed guards, I saw he was carrying the two envelopes. He was taken into a small hut and after a short time inside he came out with a soldier who waved to his men to open the barrier, we was waved through with great speed as the soldier Dion was speaking to was shouting for people to move out of the way and let us through.

We were now in Angola and straight away I sensed the change in atmosphere, there were burned out cars on the side of the road and buildings in decay, we drove a few hundred yards ill Dion pulled over and stopped besides a Mercedes jeep with two men sitting inside, Dion said a few words and the jeep pulled forward and Dion waved out his window for us to follow.

We made a few turns through the small town where I noticed a dead dog on the road, there was hardly anyone around and there was an eerie feel to the place, I never liked it as I never felt at ease at all.

Soon we drove into the open countryside where we drove onto a dirt road., we headed into the wilderness and drove for a couple of hours, we past lots of burnt out cars and a few which were obviously blown up by cannon fire or tank fire.

After a while we stopped in a small valley where I couldn't believe what I saw when we pulled over, behind us and hidden in the trees was a crashed fighter jet, it had obviously been there for some time as it was covered in weeds and parts of it were rusting.

"Cuban." One of the men said smiling as he noticed me looking at it.

I then noticed a small hut besides some tress where a man suddenly appeared with no top on just a red pair of shorts and sandals and he was holding a AK47 rifle, he walked over to the two men and Dion and after a few spoken words he went back into the hut and then came out holding some walkie talkies and the rifle.

Dion shook the hands of the two men who had drove us here and this stranger got into the passenger side of Dion's jeep, Dion then walked over to me and leant in the window.

"stay together, we are going to travel across a very dangerous part of the country, drive where I drive as there are landmines everywhere."

Before long we were back into the dirt road driving through the bush, it was very difficult staying close to Dion as the dust his jeep was making was seriously affecting my view. It was a horrible drive where I was concentrating every second just to stay close on a very dusty and bumpy road.

After another couple of hours drive I started to notice the landscape changing. Soon we were driving amongst trees and hills and before long we pulled into a compound. I followed Dion closely where I quickly noticed we had drove into a rebel militia base.

Dion pulled over and pulled up beside him now fully aware that we were surrounded by dozens of men with guns, some were dressed in military trousers but everyone was carrying guns.

The man jumped out the passenger side of Dion's jeep and walked into a hut as Dion walked back over to me now followed by over a dozen men who were looking at us and checking out the vehicles.

I was in a different world now and I fucking admit I was feeling very worried but I was trying my hardest not to look worried as the rebels studied us.

I got out next to Dion and lit up a fag and sat down on a small log. One of the men walked over with a rifle over his shoulder and pointed to my cigarette, gesturing me if I had one, I never understood at first but then said yes and I reached into my pocket to get him one but before I could give him someone shouted at him. He turned to see this older more menacing looking man walking over quickly still shouting so i backed away slightly readying myself cos I couldn't tell if he was shouting at me or the man asking for a cigarette.

The man shouted again and then pulled out a handgun and smashed the man who asked me for a cigarette round the face with it, he then shouted at the other men who was standing around us before they all quickly walked away.

I then noticed a man walk out the hut who was obviously the man in charge, he walked over to Dion embraced him and we were all invited into the hut.

When we were inside we was offered whiskey or coffee, I took a glass of whiskey and then we all sat down where Dion opened an envelope which was full of $100 bills. The chief counted the money and then Dion threw the keys of the two jeeps on to the table. The chief then gestured someone who walked across the room with a cigar box and placed it on the table. He opened the box and then took out a small handful of diamonds which looked like pieces of melted glass to me.

Brian then moved forward and started to examine the stones

"What is this shit!" Brian said sighing and sitting back in his chair.

The chief then started to argue with one of his men before turning back to Brian.

"these are good!" he said sternly

"they are shit! .. this was not what we had last time!" Brian shouted back at him as he got to his feet and grabbed the keys to the jeep..

"Dion! We go!" he then added looking at Dion, before the chief spoke again.

"Sit down! Where do you think you will go? What you go home with noting!" the chief said now himself raising his voice.

"yes! We go home with nothing and our bosses then do business with other."

"No, No , No.. we have agreement, we do business with each other."

"this shit is not business! I cannot go home to my people with this, you know who we are! The people in Johannesburg will not be pleased with this!" Brian added.

The chief then sat back and looked Brian long and hard before reaching into his pocket and pulling out a large pouch.

"arr so after you try to fuck us now you find the goods! Brian said angry.

"please calm down, you get to excited... take a look, see we can still do business." Answered the chief.

"You are fucking crook!" Brian said as he started to look at the contents of the pouch, "you must think all us fucking white boys are fools!" he added in a tone of voice which was making me feel very anxious.

"take your pick... we get more stones anyway, as much as you want!" said the chief looking a bit embarrassed and pissed off.

Brian studied the stones in silence making two stacks as he looked at them.

"We take these!" Brian then said pointing at the larger stack.

Then another man walked over and started to speak with the chief, he was shouting and pointing at the stack which became obvious he was arguing at the amount Brian had chosen.

"what is his problem?" Brian then said strongly pointing at the man.

"Take them!" the chief just replied before getting up from his chair as the man with him continued to complain, the chief shouted back and the man once again started to point at the table and us before the chief slapped him very hard around the face. The man fell to the ground and the chief kicked him on the floor before pulling out a gun and letting off two shots near the man's legs.

I jumped back not knowing what was going to happen next but the chief just carried on shouting at the man on the ground. Dion then got up and said let's go like he had seen all this before.

"get your man to take us back!" Dion then said to the chief who calmed down in an instant.

We all got back in the jeep Cherokee with Dion driving and the guide beside him in the passenger seat and me and Brian jumped in the back, as we drove out I won't say I breathed a big sigh of relief, that was an experience to say the least.

Brian was very pleased with himself and he patted my knee in excitement, "we did good, we did good.!" He whispered as he clenched his fist.

That was my first taste of Angola, dangerous as fuck and another world, it took us another three days to get home but it was exciting, I had just gone into a war zone and came out with a successful business deal…. I was fucking buzzing and rest assured, Angola was going to see me again.

Back in JO'BURG

Shai was over the moon when we returned with his bag of goodies, we had done very well and he rewarded us all with another £1000 each. Me and Dion went straight on the piss and we took a drive up to Sun City, the mini Las Vegas of Africa.

Sun city was a mini paradise stuck in the middle of nowhere in Transvaal which was real Afrikaans country. Sol Kerzner the flamboyant hotelier created the resort, it was way over the top in places but Sun City was good fun.

Me and Dion partied for a couple of days before we headed back to Jo'Burg where Shai and Andrew Pinaar had some more work for us.

We met Shai the following day at his home where he told us we would have to go with him to a place called Kimberley where me and Dion were to dress as security guards. Shai had found someone who he convinced that he could buy cheap diamonds from the De Beers mine regions of Kimberley. The plan was for the fella he found to come to the mine region with his money in the night and buy some diamonds which had been smuggled out by the workers. Shai would be at the meeting and ask the man to put down his money but before the transaction could take place, me and Dion and a couple of others would burst into the room dressed as mine security and throw Shai onto the floor, we would then drag the man we were robbing outside but once outside we would have another guy who would screech up in a car, which would make us think we were under attack so we would let the man go. We would then run into the room and pull our guns as the man who pulled up in the car would shout for the man to get in, he would then say he is a friend of Shai's and ask what happened.

His job would then be to drive the man away and drop him off saying he going back to see what happened to Shai.

Dion originally wanted me to be the driver but Shai said no as it would be difficult because of my accent and the fact I never spoke Afrikaans, this was also a very dangerous part of the robbery as the man could smell something was wrong and take the driver hostage.

But Shai was very clever as he thought of this and arranged to have two more people up the road so if something like this went wrong then the driver would drive to the other men who would do whatever they had to do get the driver away.

The next day we left for Kimberley which was a few hours' drive from Johannesburg, there was me and Dion and Shai in one car and a 4x4 with five people following us.

When we reached Kimberley, we booked into a motel and met in one room, we had the security uniforms so we got changed into them and waited for Shai to come back.

Dion then opened a bag with the guns and handed me a handgun and the pump shotgun and when Shai came back we jumped into the cars and drove into the bush for about 45 minutes.

I was buzzing and Dion handed me a bottle of whiskey which I took a large gulp of, I found myself thinking that this was a million miles away from London life but it was becoming natural to me now and anyway once I had that pump shotgun in my hands I felt fucking invincible.

We stopped at an old building near the mines, we had a quick look around and then decided where we would burst in and then Shai looked at his watch and told us to leave.

There was an old barn at the back of the building so me and Dion walked over and hid We waited in the dark until we saw a car pull up and then we crept over to the building, we could see Shai in the window with the man and we watched outside till we saw the man put the money on the table. "let's go." I said to Dion, who cocked his gun.

Moments later we burst into the room shouting and screaming with guns drawn, just as we rehearsed, Shai started to shout back at us so me and Dion grabbed him and threw him on the ground, I made out I hit Shai with the butt of the shotgun and Shai quickly saw what I did and screamed out. Dion then grabbed the man and dragged him outside into the hall and we heard the car screech up, I lowered my gun and walked over to the window to see if everything was going to plan but as I looked out I saw another car speed up the road and screech to halt, three men then jumped out and just started to fucking let their guns go!

"FUCK!" I shouted as the door I was standing next got sprayed with bullets, Dion ran over and emptied his clip out the door as Shai was grabbing the money, we ran into another room towards the back of the house as we hard machine gun fire now spraying the front door of the property.

This was well on top now so we had no choice other than run the fuck away, we had handguns and shotguns but they had Fucking machine guns and we didn't fancy those odds.

We burst into the back garden and ran towards the barn where our car was parked but as we got there we realised we never had the bloody keys, I turned around and let a couple of shots go towards the house as we heard another spray of bullets coming our way, my heart was bursting but I remember laughing as I looked at Shai who was running like an Olympic sprinter.

With no keys we couldn't use the car so we just ran into the bush, running as fast as we could we ran into the night. We could hear the guns behind still being fired but in the dark they couldn't see where went, we ran for ages until we couldn't run no more. Dion was the first to stop as he called out, he was fucked.

"FUCK THESE ARSHOLES!" he shouted as he collapsed.

I stopped and came back and kneeled beside him and grabbed his arm trying to get my breath as I looked back at where we had just ran from.

"I think we are alright." I said quietly as I couldn't see anyone.

Shai then came over and kneeled down beside me

"have you any bullets, I'm out. "he said

"What the fuck was that!" I asked angrily as I handed him my automatic. Shai smiled and shrugged, "I think they was ripping us off." He said still smiling.

"where is the money?" Dion asked

"don't worry." Shai grinned. "You don't think I left it do you."

we stayed hidden in the bush for about an hour as we could still see cars in the distance driving up and down the roads, we were in the middle of nowhere so we suspected the cars had to be the guys Shai had just robbed. It was now coming up to midnight and now the adrenaline was fading away I started to think about our predicament, we were stuck in the middle of the bush in the pitch black with a whole host of dangerous animals around us, snakes, cheetahs, even lions. Plus, a couple of cars full of men with machine guns looking for us... I remember sitting down and starting to laugh.

"what is so funny?" Dion asked me

"are you bloody kidding! I'm just sitting here wondering what the fuck am I doing in this place, if I don't get shot tonight then I'll probably get killed by a fucking snake or eaten by a lion! ..... you don't find that funny Dion?" I said back to him.

"you are crazy my brother!" Dion said back to me now laughing himself. "just stand your ground if a lion comes, don't worry they won't attack!" he added.

"stand my ground! Are you fucking serious, IL just stand here if a fucking elephant or rhino comes flying at me ..... IL fucking shoot it! I said back to him.

"stop your moaning you two." Shai then said to us.

"so what's the plan?" I then asked Shai who laying down on his back looking like he never had a care in the world.

"we sleep here till morning, maybe things will be a bit quieter then." he said as he pulled out his mobile phone.

"call Eric." I said talking about one of the men who came with us and was driving.

"Eric doesn't have a cell phone." Shai said

I then noticed Dion lay down which made me realise what we were doing.

"I'm not fucking sleeping here all night!" I said now feeling worried.

"Don't worry we will be fine, the animals will not come near us, they are more scared of us." Answered Dion

"animals! What about the fucking snakes, scorpions?" I replied "you have two choices Joe, sleep here or go back to the road and take your chances with the machine guns." Replied Shai.

Fucking great! I thought as I hesitantly lowered myself on the ground. That night I hardly slept at all as all could hear was movement of animals all through the night, ironically I was just going into a deep sleep just as the bloody sun rose. i closed my eyes again but kept being attacked by the biggest bloody flies you had ever seen, so I thought sod this and just sat up and looked over to Shai and Dion who were still sleeping like babies, I was covered in bites and dying for a drink, I actually felt sick from thirst. I reached over and gave Dion a firm push to wake him up.
The rest of the day a bloody nightmare, we got up and staying close to the road began our walk towards Kimberley, which was about twenty odd miles away. I was fucking dying as the sun hit midday, it had now been over 16 hours since we had a drink and we were getting burned to fuck walking under the sun.
After a couple of more hours we reached a small railway station and when the station guard saw us he couldn't believe how we looked, we quickly got something to drink and washed in the small bathroom and then asked about the next train.
"you have missed the train." Answered the guard
"so when is the next one coming?" I asked him
"tomorrow morning."
"WHAT!" I snapped back at him.
"we have one train a day come through here, I was just going home." The guard answered looking eager to get off.
Shai then sighed and spoke.
"get us to Jo'Burg and you can have 500 rand." He said which made the guards face light up.
500 rand was around £100 which was probably twice or three times what the guard was earning a month so he didn't take much convincing to help.
"do you have a car?" Shai added
"no, sir, but my uncle does."
"where is your uncle."

"in the town 5 kilometres from here."

"go and get him then!" Dion added sternly.

The guard didn't need asking twice and he quickly pulled out an old push bike and flew off up the road like he was in a race.

A short while after this old Datsun pulled up with the guard and another man driving.

"will that make it to fucking Jo'Burg?" I asked looking at the state of the car.

The trip back was bloody awful and took hours as the driver wouldn't drive over 30 mph! we were driving on long roads through the bush with no other cars and this dope wouldn't drive faster, it was bloody arduous cramped up in the back with Dion and bloody sweltering.

when Shai got a signal on his phone he called home to find his wife worried sick as Eric and the four other men had returned to Jo'Burg and gone straight to Shai's home in there 4x4 which was riddled with bullets.

When we got back to Shai's house I couldn't believe the state of the car as there must have been a hundred holes in it and it was a miracle no one was killed never mind shot! We walked straight into the garden where the men were sitting eating, we grabbed a drink off the table and sat down, we were absolutely filthy from all the red dust of the bush, lady Jan was also there and she looked relived I was back safe.

Dion then grabbed Eric and pushed him up against a wall and shouted at him for leaving us.

"WE CAME BACK FOR YOU!" Eric shouted

"YOU LEFT US IN THE FUCKING BUSH!" Dion said as he squeezed Eric's throat only for Shai to tell Dion to leave it.

"what happened?" Shai than said to Eric.

"we did what you asked Shai and pulled up outside the house but a car followed us and started shooting, we had to drive off! We drove away and then came back and chased the men away, we then went into the house and you were gone, we searched all through the night for you." Eric answered frantically, "we wouldn't leave you!" he added looking at Dion.

"you fucking lie, we saw them driving up and down the road for hours!"
Dion said.
"that was us bro, we chased them off and they drove off towards
Kimberley! We must have drove around for an hour looking for you but we
had to go as we knew the cops might come."

I looked across at Dion who looked at me and I gave him a look to say it
sounds okay.
"so they just started firing first?" Dion then asked.
"Yar! They must have been parked just off the road watching their man's
back, they never even put their lights on, we pulled up and before we could
even get out we were shot at."
"and then you drove off and left us?" Dion added
"We had no choice bro! we were sitting ducks so we sped off and then
turned around and came back but once we started shooting at them they
fucked off!"
We sat around and talked for a few more minutes before I walked off for a
shower, the dust that Came off me was unreal, it was in my ears and my
hair it was everywhere.
I got out the shower and then put a towel around my waist and then
suddenly noticed I was being watched so I turned around and saw lady Jan
standing there in the bathroom.
"I was worried about you." She said walking over and rubbing my back
letting her hand drop so it touched my arse.
"Fuck!" I remember thinking as I felt myself getting embarrassed.
"did you hurt yourself?" she then added as she moved her hand across my
stomach and pushed her fingers down into the towel.
It was a very strange situation to be in as my head went into overdrive, I
was thinking get me out of here and then I thought, sod it! Shall I just throw
her on the sink and bang the arse of her.
 She moved closer and then I just freaked, I pulled away all embarrassed
and made up some silly excuse about not feeling too well, she got the
message and backed off now herself looking slightly embarrassed.
"il be downstairs in a minute Jan." I said as she moved towards the door.

Fucking hell that was a lucky escape, I thought. Thinking back on it don't know if that moment scared me more than the men coming at me with machine guns!

Downstairs I found Shai and Dion sitting alone as Eric and the others had left, they were smoking a joint and counting the money on the table. It was a good result as there was 90000 rand which was around £25000.
Shai took 50000 rand for himself and then pushed 25000 over towards me and Dion.
"you two take twenty-five, IL spit the rest with the others." Shai said which made Dion sit up and smile as our original share was going to be 10000 rand.
"are you sure?" Dion asked
"yes, take it, you two deserve it more than the others." Answered Shai

So it was a job well done and later that night when we went back to Dion's we both had our pockets full of money, I put it in the room with the money I had left from Angola which beginning to add up nicely.
I was still pumped from the night before, I knew what I was doing was dangerous, even crazy but when you looked at the, money it made it all worth it.
South Africa was a fun place to be, I didn't admit but looking back at it I was having the time of my life.

P.E (Port Elizabeth)

Port Elizabeth or commonly just known as PE was one of the largest cities in south Africa situated on the coast about a thousand kilometres from Johannesburg.

A couple of days after the Kimberley job, Dion got a phone call from some of his old army pals in PE.

They had some work for him so Dion said that we would go down there to see them.

The following day we jumped on a plane and took the hour and a half flight down to the sea-coast town.

PE was really nice, it had a fantastic beach and was much different from the urban city of Jo'Burg, it had that holiday feel to it. We booked into a small hotel by the seafront and later in the night Dion's friends came over to see us and we all went out for a meal.

We were then told about a problem his friends were having with some rivals in the local 'Mandrex' trade.

Mandrax or Mandrex was absolutely huge in south Africa, it was a synthetic drug which was crushed and smoked usually in a cannabis joint. The market was huge in south Africa and again for libel reasons I won't say I know anything but I heard that many people on the fringes of the ANC got very very rich in the Mandrax trade.

Anyway these pals of Dion had just had a 'parcel' taken off them from a gang of locals who were now threatening everyone that they must buy the Mandrex off them instead. This gang was a real bunch of slags as they threatened to kill Dion's pals but then called the cops when they made a meeting to have a fight.

Fucking scumbags, they rob you and then try to get you nicked, these were the kind of people I detested, no morals and no bollocks.

"so what is you want?" Dion asked one of them

"this piece of shit must go!" replied one of his friends talking about their rival gang leader.

"what's stopping you then?" asked Dion

"the cops, they will know it is us now, when we went to the fight the cops were there waiting for us, they arrested us and now if anything happens to these bastards then they will come straight for us." His friend replied "we all have to have cast iron alibis." He added.

Dion then looked at me, "do you fancy this bro?" he asked raising his eye brows.

I just shrugged as if to say maybe, what's it worth.

Dion then turned back his friend, "okay we can do this, but it won't be cheap, you are my friend but this is your fucking problem and not mine, it is business so if you want my help then it will be a business matter and not a matter of brothers."

"of course, this I understand." The man answered.

"then tell me bro, how much is it worth to you for this man to no longer be a problem?" Dion asked him.

"we will pay twenty thousand rand."

"twenty thousand! Are you fucking crazy or something? You earn that in one week! Its fifty thousand and this problem of yours is over … very quickly!" Dion snapped back.

Dion's friend smiled slightly, "how quickly?" he asked

"24 hours!" Dion answered.

The man thought for a second and then held out his hand, "okay, let's do this." He said firmly.

"I will need a car and the tools and addresses." Dion then added.

Later that night me and Dion sat having a beer while talking about the job, I was still a bit unsure but I was in way too deep now, there was no way I could start making excuses or looking worried.

"so what are we going to do, put this man in hospital?" I asked although I knew what the reply would be.

"Fuck the hospital, we send this clown to hell!"

"why don't we call Shai and Andrew and get someone down here from Jo'Burg? Let someone else do the work." I suggested.

"No, Joe, its easy work, this is much easier than what we went through in Kimberley or Angola, me and you do it bro and we keep all the money, you drive and I will go to his door and do it"

The next morning, we woke early and went downstairs to have some breakfast, I remember feeling a bit hesitant and I was wanting to say to Dion that I didn't fancy doing this job. The work didn't put me off but the principle did, I never knew these people or their backgrounds.

I sat at the breakfast table eating bacon and eggs in near silence as I mulled over the day we had ahead of us. I was very conflicted but I couldn't back out as it would make me look like a coward or weak.

Half way through our breakfast we were joined by Dion's pals who handed us a small bag with a polaroid picture and two hand guns.

We had a brief chat where they gave us an address and then left us sitting there with the bag.

What happened that day or all the time I was in Port Elizabeth was a time I am not proud of, the next few hours were not what I call my finest hours and I will leave it up to you to make your own minds up.

There are two possible outcomes...

We took the money and did the job!

Or we took the money and just fucked off back to Jo'Burg knocking dion's pals

Let's just say it by evening we were flying back to Jo'Burg with a lot more money in our pockets than what we had on us when we arrived.

Making Plans

Once back in Blairgowie, me and Dion spent the rest of the week having fun, we did a few little jobs for Shai, just driving jobs but we spent most of the time drinking and having fun.

I was also pondering on what I was doing out here and where it was all leading, I was getting deeper and deeper into the Johannesburg underworld and getting involved in some serious work, lady Jan had been on the phone a couple of times asking me to come to work at the warehouse but I was now too embedded into the schemes of Shai and Dion to spend time with Jan. Shai was also opening up to me and telling things I really didn't want to know. Shai was a born con man, like so many other south Africans at that time, he just lived to fuck people over.

Shai is dead now, I found out a couple of years ago but he wasn't that old so I don't think it was from natural causes.

When I think back now I can see that life was cheap in Jo'Burg and people like Shai and Dion lived their lives almost knowing that they would not live a long life. They had a strange outlook on life which was to cram as much in as quick as you can and don't give a fuck. Shai was crazy, he just didn't care who he ripped off, he lived like he had a death wish.

One time in Africa I got involved with some very infamous English mercenaries and I was the middle man for a deal between them and people connected to the ANC, it was a big deal worth a lot of money and then I found out the mercenaries were working with or for the American CIA. I went straight to Shai and told him what I knew, I was worried about my safety as the meeting was set for Soweto, a place I hated going to. Introducing Shai and his associates to the CIA was a problem, especially if they thought I knew they were CIA. That day when I went to Soweto, I was genuinely worried that I would never return. It was a strange place for Shai to ask me to meet him as I knew that many people who go to Soweto never

come out. When I told Shai the news he just smiled and said to me, "I know who they are, do you not think we have ways to find out."
I was relieved and I also said we should scrap the deal and walk away but Shai wasn't hearing it, he was now wanting to rip the people off, that how fearless or stupid he was, he was going to rip the CIA and mercenaries off. now I'm involved up to my neck, if he rips them off then I'm the link and I'm the man they will come for. Luckily the deal never happened anyway, the mercenary who was once a Major got involved in a big trial in the UK. I later found out he was working for Special branch as well as the CIA and was setting people up. The rats name was Major John Banks.

I had now been in South Africa for quite some time and it was a mixture of danger and partying like mad, one night we had some fun in the local bar where Dion decided to get his maid drunk when we came back to the house. There was a few of us drinking and cheering her on as she stripped in the garden, when she took her top off I almost choked on my beer as she had huge tits shaped like two rugby balls. Dion was blind drunk walking over to her and grabbing them which made all of us laugh. It was a great party that night apart from me being bitten by a snake in the garden.
I remember thinking fuck I am in trouble; it was only a small snake which clamped its mouth on my wrist when I sat down on the grass. I quickly pulled the snake off and threw it onto the ground where it got stamped on by everyone shouting and jumping around.
Dion then ran over to me, "Shit bro, you're in fucking trouble!" he shouted looking serious.
"what! What does that mean." I answered thinking the worst
"that fucker is going to kill you!"
"then get me to the fucking hospital!" I shouted back at him as ii felt my pulse start to race.
"it's up the road, ten-minute walk bro."
"walk! Are you fucking mad, drive me to the fucking hospital!"
"I've just opened a beer!" Dion replied which made the others start to laugh

"You cunt!" I said now laughing, "it's not poisonous is it" I added looking at the others.

I felt angry at first and then relieved as someone walked over to me and handed me another beer, "it's a house snake." He said smiling.

"it's not poisonous?" I asked

"No! Drink it's not venomous." He said which made think thank god.

The Phone call..

A couple of days after my escapade with the snake me and Dion were sitting in the garden one morning when we had a phone call from the two Rhodesian mercenaries we met on the border of Angola.

They were in Johannesburg and wanted to see us.

We set a meeting up for the following day as we were busy that day running some errands for Andrew Pinaar.

I remember feeling hesitant about meeting the two strangers as we didn't really know anything about them, they seemed like nice fellas when we had a few beers with them but I knew they wasn't calling us for a beer.

The next day we met them in a small Irish bar in the district of Hilbrow.

We had a couple of lagers and then found out what they wanted to see us about. They were travelling back up to the border and was interested in the jeeps they saw us in when we met them there before. They guessed they were stolen and they said if we take two or three of them back to Oshiknago they would give us cash for them in Namibia or if we wanted to drive into Angola we could swap them for diamonds.

I was hesitant with working with them as I never trusted mercenaries, to me they were men for sale, men who didn't care what side they fought on so long as they got paid. Dion however was buzzing!

For ages Dion was always moaning saying Shai was probably getting a fortune for the stones we brought back to him and now this was a chance for him to get his own diamonds.

That night when we got back to Dion's he wasted no time calling his friends about getting his hands on a couple of jeeps, I sat down in the front room listening to the phone call still not relishing the prospect of working with these people.

"so are we doing it?" I asked as he put the phone down.

"we would be crazy not to!" he replied as lit up a joint.

"what do we really know about these men?" I asked trying to talk him out of it.

"Arr, don't worry they are good men! They are like us; the Rhodesians are men of their word!"

"we should check them out mate."

"with who? Shai? Andrew? If we do that then we let everyone know what we are doing!"

"Dion, I don't fancy going into Angola with these people, they're into guns' mate." I added saying what I suspected that the men were gun traders.

"what's the matter with you?" Dion then asked looking at me strangely.

"don't tell me you're fucking scared Joe!" he added

"what's fucking scared got to do with anything! I'm thinking more about being fucking idiots!"

"Arr.... you think too much! Its easy fucking work, trust me, I will make sure everything is okay."

"how the fuck are you going to do that?" I snapped back now feeling pissed off.

"what has got into you? I have never seen you speak this way..... look if you do not want to drive into Angola then I will drive myself, me and Johnny." Dion replied mentioning Johnny who was a local lad we sometimes drank with and was a fucking idiot.

I shook my head and laughed which annoyed Dion.

"if you don't want to do it because you're scared then stay here and work with lady Jan, go back to the fucking warehouse that she brought you over for."

"I aint fucking scared!" I snapped back before getting to my feet.

"what are you doing?" Dion said as got up.

"going to fucking bed, we're talk in the morning when we're sober!"

Angola Hell

That night I laid in bed thinking I should just pack my bags and get on the first flight to London. Things were getting out of control now and I could just feel what we were doing was not right.

It felt like I was now in a world which was getting more dangerous by the day. I wish I would have listened to the voices in my head.

A few days later we were once again on the road in two stolen jeeps and travelling to the Angolan border, me Dion and that fucking idiot Johnny. When we reached the border town of Oshiknago we met the mercenaries who then took us to a small farm on the outskirts of the town. We parked the two jeeps in a barn where I noticed a large truck which was being guarded by a few men. In fact, the barn was swarming with other Rhodesian men.

I was still hoping that we would sell the jeeps but I knew Dion was really excited about getting his hands on some rough cut stones.

We went into the barn and I had a wash before we sat down and had a beer. Dion was already in discussion when I came back from the bathroom, already talking about going back into Angola.

I listened in silence as they spoke and found out it was guns they were taking into Angola the next day, they had been doing this for some time now and on the last trip they were asked to bring jeeps or cars the next time they came.

"Why don't we give you the cars here and you bring us back some stones?" I suddenly said which made Dion look at me with a look like I said something wrong.

"Why would we do that?" answered the mercenary. "we are giving you the option to take a bite from our plate, you take money now or come with us and do your own business with the stones! For us it would be better to give you money here." he added.

"No we come with you!" Dion then answered.

"Where are going to?" I asked

"just south of Xangongo!"

"how far is that?"

"it was Swapo land, two hours' drive north."

Fucking Swapo land! That meant nothing to me except I knew Angola was kicking off all over the place. MPLA who were the new formed government were fighting UNITA again after decades of war, a war which saw so many different countries involved in including Cuba, the Soviet Union and south Africa.

The next morning, we left for the border in a convoy of five vehicles and the truck. We crossed into Angola without any problems, I was driving one jeep with Dion in the passenger seat and Johnny was driving the other jeep behind.

The plan was to follow the convoy to where they were going where after they did their business we would exchange the two jeeps for diamonds and then jump in with the mercenaries for a lift back to Namibia.

(I am calling them the mercenaries because I do not want to say their names)

After a couple of hours drive we reached the town of Xangongo, it was a quite a large town but was very battle scarred, everywhere around us were destroyed buildings and burnt out cars. We pulled up to a small encampment where the convoy stopped and one of the mercenaries got out his car and walked back to us.

"Wait here, put your cars over there and wait!" he said firmly and pointing.

I pulled the jeep over besides a large steel shack and reversed it just under a tree in the shade as we watched the convoy drive off.

"what are we doing Dion?" I asked as this was making me feel bloody nervous.

"waiting!" Dion replied looking as freaked out as I was feeling.

We stayed where we was for over an hour where I suggested we just fuck off, this wasn't the plan and people were walking past us and looking at us sitting there, three white men in two shiny new jeeps parked in some fucking alley in a bloody war zone.

Dion looked like he was just about to agree when something happened that that sent a feeling through me I will never forget.

Three military vehicles suddenly screeched down the alley where a dozen soldiers jumped out pointing AK47's at us, they shouted for us to get out and then the madness started.

Dion got out first and kneeled down with his hands on his head and I followed what he did, the soldiers then ran over and I was kicked to the ground and hit with the butt of the gun on the side of my head, my whole head began to buzz as ringing went through my ears. My face was pushed down into the dirt and felt the warm blood pour down into my eyes and face. The next thing I remember was a loud thud and I was knocked out.

I awoke in dirty corrugated steel cell which was unbearably hot and my head was thumping, I knew I was concussed as I remember having the craziest half dreams when I was in and out of consciousness.

My body ached all over and I had scratches all over my hands arms and legs and was bleeding from everywhere it seemed.

The feeling I had was a strange one as I was heavily concussed, I was scared but because my head was buzzing it just didn't seem real what was happening to me.

Before long I heard the door open and three men grabbed me and dragged me out the cell by my feet. I was taken to adjacent building where I was put in a room with just a chair in the middle of the room.

After a short while two men came in with the soldiers who dragged me there. I was pulled up and placed on the chair where the two men, one in civilian clothes and the other in uniform spoke to me but I never understood what they were saying or what language they were talking in.

"I don't understand." I said back to them.

"you are south African!" the civilian then said before talking to the other man as they both pointed at me and strangely enough my hair which was short at the time.

"you are not south African!" the man who spoke before said.

"No." I said "I'm English."

"English! and you are in Angola!" the man said before once again talking to the other man before they both walked out the room leaving me on my own with the soldiers.

I was left like this for what seemed like hours, I aching everywhere and my head was killing me and everything was still hazy, my mouth was dry and I never had a clue where I was or how long I had been here. I remember asking one of the soldiers for some water only to be ignored.

I was also drifting in and out of sleep as I was exhausted. I thought about getting on the floor and lying down but I knew the soldiers wouldn't allow it.

I was just on the brink of sleep again when the door opened and the two men walked in with another man only this man was white but he was olive skinned, like Spanish or something.

One of the soldiers walked out and quickly came back in with a chair for him and then sat down opposite me.

"what are you doing here?" he asked speaking very good English but with a hint of an accent which I later found out was Cuban.

My head was killing me and I didn't know what to say so I just shrugged and looked at him

"you are a mercenary are you not? Maybe ex English army…. Is that correct?" he then said to me which sent my mind into chaos.

"No I'm not!" I replied quickly.

"then what are you doing in Angola?" he asked again.

"I don't know." I remember saying which made him lean forward and grab my bollocks really hard

"WHAT ARE YOU DOING HERE!" he then shouted as two soldiers grabbed my arms and pulled them behind my back.

The man then slapped me hard around the face which made my head buzz again. He must have hit me a few times because the next thing I remember is waking up in the steel cell again.

I tried to sit up but I was in agony, my head was still killing me and I was seeing double vison, I was only awake a few moments when the door opened and a soldier handed me some water and then slammed the door shut again.

I remember now the feeling I had when I drank the water, it was the best drink I have ever had. I sat back and tried to steady myself in my small cell. The cell was tiny, it was about five foot by four foot and I couldn't stretch out fully. It was made of four panels of that corrugated steel stuff with just a dirt floor and a large piece of wood for the roof. It was also situated in the open grounds or courtyard of the military camp where I was.

Inside the cell it was sweltering hot, it was so hot I could hardly breathe and the sweat was dripping off me constantly.

My head was fucking throbbing still where everything was hazy, I knew I was in load of trouble but I was like a dream just going from one nightmare to another.

Outside I could hear loads of people and vehicles coming and going and I found a few gaps around the nails where I could look out.

I was left for a few hours until once again as it was getting dark I was dragged back into the room with the chair in it. This time my hands were tied behind my back and was blindfolded and just left there in the dark for a few hours.

When the door opened I noticed the light switched on and I heard footsteps, they took off my blindfold which hurt my eyes and then the Cuban grabbed my face.

"we know everything." He said pushing my head back

I then noticed the door open where three soldiers were holding Johnny outside in the corridor, he was bloodied and unconscious, the door was then shut and the Cuban turned back to me.

"who were you meeting?" I remember him asking me.

Now remember I never had a fucking clue who we were meeting so how can I answer him. I thought for a moment and then answered the only way I could.

"I don't know who." I answered only to be hit hard around the face with an open hand.

My head twisted to side making my neck hurt as he hit me a few more times.

"I DON'T FUCKING KNOW!" I said feeling angry, scared and frustrated.

The Cuban then took a handgun out and pushed it into my face. I closed my eyes and thought he was going to shoot me. The gun was pushed hard into my cheek which forced my head to turn to the side and then all of a sudden the man just got up, said a few things to one of the soldiers and then walked out the room.

I was left like this all night with two soldiers who I found out were ordered not to let me sleep as every time I closed my eyes they walked over and slapped me hard around the face. That night was agony, I could barely keep my eyes open, I was exhausted both mentally and physically. I sat in that fucking room all night long not being allowed to sleep with my arms cramping up from being tied behind my back.

When daylight broke the door was opened and the two soldiers who had been watching me and hitting me all night were replaced by two other soldiers, one soldier looked around fifteen. They walked over to me and removed all my clothes with a knife so I was sitting there completely naked still tied to the chair.

I looked up at the young soldier who was just looking at me, I can still remember his face and expression now, he was completely emotionless, just staring at me blankly.

The door opened again and two more men walked in where I was blindfolded once again, a moment later some liquid was thrown over me which smelt like petrol or gasoline, I remember it burning me as it went down to my legs. I was left like this until I heard footsteps and then I felt them un tie my arms and tie my ankles as I was being held.

I was then dragged out the room into the yard where I was forced on my knees where they placed my hands on my head and untied my blindfold. The sun hurt my eyes and then I saw two soldiers standing in front of me pointing their rifles towards my face. My head just fucking spun as this was it I thought, I'm being shot.

One of the men who had interrogated me earlier then shouted at the soldiers who both tensed and aimed at my face. My mind just went blank and I closed my eyes as the man shouted and then I heard two clicks.

I then heard laughter as I opened my eyes to see about a dozen men laughing at me.

I was then quickly grabbed and once again thrown into my cell hard banging my head against the wall.

During the rest of the day I started to get angry. It's a funny thing but I don't know if this is normal for interrogation but once I was broken I found myself not giving a fuck, something inside me just snapped as the thought of death didn't seem too bad. As I sat there in the sweltering heat I found myself wanting them to come back for me. It was the solitude that was the most painful now, the feeling of waiting... I found myself saying "JUST FUCKING DO IT!"

Something deep inside of me just turned on where they had done their worst, I had been beaten for at least two days, had a mock execution, so what the fuck else could they do to me. I actually found myself wanting them to hit me again.

Every fucking part of me ached, my stomach was killing me from hunger and the dehydration and concussion was making me feel drowsy, barely able to stay awake, which in hindsight was probably a good thing now.

Time was another thing I had no account for, obviously I knew when it was day and night but I just couldn't think straight, I never knew how many days I had been there or even cared.

I think I was left for a couple of days where the bastards gave me water and some rice a few times, I remember a cut on my arm which was really hurting and it was infected as it swelled up really bad. It hurt and it was difficult to keep it clean on the dusty floor where I lay naked.

My face was also swollen and my left eye was still half closed from a large bump just above my brow.

It was horrible just being there not knowing what the fuck was going on, I never knew what was going to happen next and every footstep near me made me tense is if they were going to open the door.

The next time I was brought out or dragged out was just before sunset. I remember looking at the camp as they walked me across the yard and I saw it was busier than usual. I was taken inside and walked into the same room where there was five men already inside. One was the Cuban but he had another Cuban with him and three soldiers.

I was sat on the chair and left there as the five men spoke amongst themselves, intermittently pointing at me, one of the Cubans also walked over and pointed at my hair and then grabbed it as he spoke to one of the men in the room.

(I never found out why they kept talking about my hair but as a guess I would say it was because most south Africans around my age at the time had longish hair while I had short hair.)

After a short while, two of soldiers who brought me into the room were ordered to tie my hands again behind my back, they did this quickly and also this time tied my ankles to the legs of the chair.

They then walked off to the side of the room as the five men who had been talking left the room. Nothing was asked of me which I remember seemed strange as I was asking myself what is going on this time.

I was left like this for a while until the two Cubans came back into the room followed by some bastard who I hadn't seen before, he was black and dressed in military pants with boots on but had a dirty white shirt on with his sleeves rolled up, he was skinny and ugly as fuck with goofy teeth, he was also carrying a small bag which he threw down at my feet making a loud bang as it hit the ground.

One of the Cubans then looked at the two soldiers in the room who walked over and grabbed my shoulders and face so I couldn't move.

The Cuban then started asking me if I knew some names he was saying, I never knew any of them, never heard of them! I can't remember the names but they sounded foreign or south African.

The bastard who came in with them then pulled out a hammer from the bag and struck me hard on the shin, the pain was really bad, agony and then he hit me on the other shin before they asked me again if I knew the names.

I never knew them so I just said NO!

The pain was so bad I was nearly passing out and the fact I couldn't move just made things worse.

The two men tightened their grip on my head where one had me in a head lock as the skinny man reached into his pocket and pulled out a large nail, it was one of those six inch nails. I remember trying to struggle but I couldn't move, they then held me so tight I almost passed out as one of them opened my mouth, pulling my jaw down, I tried to bite his fingers but I just couldn't get the strength, the bastard then pushed the nail into my mouth still holding onto it and then he hit the nail with the hammer and I felt the most fucking horrible pain I had ever felt in my life, the nail entered my gum on the side just under one of my back teeth, it was agony.

Somehow I managed to move and the nail fell out onto the floor, all I remember then is the room going blurry where the next thing I remember is waking up back in my stinking cell.

I woke up once again in pain but I was getting really fucked off now, remember I knew nothing, all I knew was we had a couple of stolen jeeps which we were trying to swap for some stones. I knew nothing about the war or guns or anything.

My body was in fucking pieces and so was my mind now, I was even thinking about just trying to end it, looking around the cell for something to just open my wrists up.

I was left for a couple of days, just lying in the dark, not knowing what was going to happen. The unknown was the killer, my mind had nothing to do except think about any moment they would open the door and drag me back into that fucking room again.

The next time they opened the cell I was pulled up on to my feet where a soldier handed me a pair of army trousers and I was also given some sandals and some water, he nodded at me to put the trousers on and then they shut the door for an hour or so.

When they opened up again they told me to put my hands behind my back and I was tied and blindfolded again. I thought they was taking me back to the room and I stopped in m tracks and said NO! but they grabbed me and took me to a vehicle where I was pushed into the back and left on the floor as they drove off.

We drove for a couple of hours with me still just lying there not having a clue what was going on. I remember the pain as I was lying on my arm, the one which was infected. I tried to move and then someone helped me move onto my other side. I felt emotional as this was the first person to show me any humanity for quite some time.

When the truck stopped I was surprised to be helped out the back of it and then walked fast but still blindfolded into a building. Once inside they took off my blindfold and I was told to wash in a shower that was in a small room, the soldier stood watch as I turned the ice cold shower on and washed away the dirt and dried blood.

I was then given some flat bread and some water and took to an iron cage which had seven other men in it.

The cage was outside but it had a wooden roof laid on top of the iron bars to shield the sun. the other men looked battered and demoralised and just looked at me not knowing what to make out of this white man being thrown into the cage with them. I saw a small space to the side and then sat down on my own.

This cage turned out to be my home for the next few weeks, where I discovered the men I was with were UNITA rebels.

They couldn't speak much English, hardly anything but they shared any food and water they had with me.

Looking back at it now, sharing this small cage with these men was utter hell but at the time and after the room back in the previous camp this was very comfortable. The men even helped me with my wounds.

The cage itself was disgusting, no toilets just a large plastic container cut in half to have a shit in. if we wanted to piss we would all go to a corner and just piss out into the dirt. It was a specific corner which we all used.

Hygiene wise it was terrible, most of us were suffering from diarrhoea and we had no toilet paper, the stink was unbearable and the large flies would fly around the container and then fly out onto your skin. Some days there would be hundreds of flies as they infested the cage. Most of the days was spent killing them as they landed but for every fly you swatted on your skin it wouldn't be long before ten or more would take its place.

One of things that strikes me was in this hell where I saw the worst kind of barbarity I also saw some of the most amazing acts of humanity. It is strange how two extremes can exist side by side.

One such act was when one of men in cage with me was bitten in the night by a scorpion or spider. Dala as I called him slept two places away from me and one night he woke up crying out. It was pitch black so no one could do anything but in the morning he showed us his leg which was starting to swell and blister. Over the next 24 hours, Dala become more and more sick, his wound got worse by the hour and the other men sat with him trying to help him. The soldiers brought us water and some leaves but they weren't allowed to open up the cage. The leaves were soaked in the water and then wrapped around his leg, one man must have held the leaves tight around his leg for hours as Dala got worse and worse and started to vomit. The next day and night was horrific as he started to go delirious, he was crying out all through the night were the other men held him and comforted him, they even lifted him and held him over the plastic container as he went to the toilet.

Poor Dala died that night, he was crying out and then just went silent. The other men chanted besides him all through the night holding him. In the morning the soldiers came over and saw he was dead but again they couldn't open the cage. Dala was left with us until the next day where his body was removed by three soldiers.

Everyone in the cage wept as they removed Dala, I was upset as well. I also remember the other men all going over to the spot where his body had been, the place where he slept where everyone took turns to kneel in his spot and say some words to the ground.

My life in the cage continued day to day exactly the same as the day before, we slept and then tried to sit out of the sun in the day until we slept again at night. I was wondering all the time what was going to happen to me, it had now been a couple of weeks since anyone had spoken to me or let out the cage to stretch my legs.

I was starting to think I would be here forever when one day I was taken into the building and told to shower. When I came out I was then given some clean army trousers and a clean shirt.

Nothing was said to me, not a word, once dressed I was taken to a Toyota open back truck and sat in the back surrounded by three soldiers. We drove for a few hours until the truck stopped and I was helped off the truck. I then turned to see we was about a hundred yards from the border of Namibia.

The soldiers then smiled at me and pointed for me to walk to the border. My head was spinning as I dared to believe I was being released. I hesitated for a moment as thought they might shoot me if I walk off but then they just got back onto the back of the truck and they started to drive off.

The feeling I had was breath taking! I turned to the border and took a few steps and then sprinted as fast as I could.

As I got there I was met by more soldiers who walked me into an office where once inside I was met by a white gentleman who was there waiting for me. I was asked a few questions and then driven south for about an hour where we got on a plane and flew to Windhoek, a few hundred kilometres south.

I was free, just like that and I didn't even have the chance to say goodbye to my friends in the cage. The white man who met me at the border told me he worked for the Namibian government and I was released as part of a deal that the government had done with Luanda, the capital of Angola. I asked him what deal and he said he couldn't say, he just replied that I was a very lucky man and that I should get back to England as quickly as possible.

When I arrived in Windhoek I was taken straight to a hotel where I met someone from the English embassy, I signed some papers and then I was taken to the airport where I was placed on a plane home.

The flight took me to Amsterdam and then from there I caught a plain back to Heathrow.

When I got to Heathrow I was taken into customs and interviewed as I never had a passport, just a piece of paper from the embassy. The police then interviewed me where I told them what happened. I was then interviewed by two senior officers who I suspect where special branch. During this interview I collapsed with exhaustion where I was rushed into hospital and placed on a drip.

They kept me in hospital for a couple of days where I was tested for aids, hepatitis and cholera.

When I got on the scales I weighed 9 and half stone! I had lost nearly three stone. Physically I recovered quickly but it took a few years to get my mind back to normal. It took a few years of sometimes waking in the sweating, thinking I was back in that cage or back in chair.

Even to this day I still don't know why I was released? Thank god I was!
A couple of years ago I tried to find out but the foreign office had no record of me in Windhoek.

It was a harrowing time but a time which is part of me, over the years it has helped me centre myself at times of trouble and made me realise just how precious life really is.

I had fun and it was an adventure but ultimately I lost out there. I was taken to a place with my body and my mind, a place very dark and a place which came as close to hell as this world can get.

I have never spoken to Dion again, I did here that he got back to Jo'Burg but my life ended in south Africa the day I came home on that flight.

Below is a poem that I wrote reflecting on my experience in south Africa, it featured in my book From Villain to Verse Maker.

Bested but not Beaten

Shackled to a chair gasping for air
Blood on the floor waiting for more
Now all alone I am hurt to the bone
Yet inside I smile
Day after day they have tortured my body
Still I am strong I have given them nobody
Cut with a knife and beaten with a stick
Russian roulette as I hear another click
Haven't seen the sun for days on end
Yet its warmth shines brightly as my honour I defend
Tell me the names of the men you protect
Punch after punch only strengthens my reject
Yesterday I was close, close to confess
Today I am past the limit, I couldn't care less
You have played your hand and given me your best
I have now come through your barbaric test
You didn't break me on the first day, now your methods have failed
The more you hit me just makes me more proud
I won't give you anything, only my scorn
Any hope you had is now forlorn
Take off my blindfold; let me see your eyes
I can taste your frustration as yourself respect dies
Hit me, strike me, let me feel another blow
But your never force me to tell you all I know
I am willing to die and go to my grave
With a smile on my face knowing friend's I have saved
Let them live long and let them be free
Let them remember the friend in me
I will rise into heaven with my soul complete
You have taken my life but yours is defeat
Open your arms to me Jesus my lord
I went out fighting holding my sword
So, who has won and who has lost
You can have my life but at what cost

You tried everything you knew to make me talk
Now get out of my way and let me walk
You're a coward, a rat, a man full of doubt
Look at me now as pride I shout
Just walk out the door and leave me alone
I am stronger than you though you've bled me to the bone
Doesn't matter anymore, anything you do
I'm willing to die as long as I'm true
You smashed me near death now you know your mistake
Two men in a room, only one man is fake
I've took your blows and took your threats
And all that you have done is learned regret
The only thing left is you'll hear me rejoice
Defiance and pride are filling my voice
I see your anger I smell your hate
But I'd rather die true than have your fate
I have won, you have lost
Now walk away and remember the cost...

Poetry
Where did it come from?

Believe it or not I first started writing verse to impress the girls, I would send them a small card and put a few words in and because of the success it gave me I must have thought I was good at it. They were short comical little pieces of rhyme, corny stuff like,

The next time I meet you can I give you a kiss
please be generous and don't take the piss
make my day and don't call me a farce
kiss my neck and pinch my arse!

It was just a bit of light-hearted fun, a bit cheeky cockney and a bit romantic.
nothing serious!
I suppose the serious side or the side of poetry that gripped me was a few years later when I was unfortunate enough to find myself in a cell in Her majesty's prison Brixton. It was 1992 and in those days, you never had TV's and 'Playstations' in your cell, you had 'Fuck all!' just a pen and paper and locked up all day to think about why you were in there.
I can remember lying in my cell and I just received a letter from Ronnie Kray and at the bottom of the page he wrote a quote from Winston Churchill.

If you're going through hell, keep going

I remember reading that small quote over and over again, I wrote it out and stuck it above my head on the bunk bed and found myself saying it loud countless times a day.
The next few days saw me get my hands on a book by Lord Alfred Tennyson. That changed my life, the words and the way he put them together just blew me away. The man was an absolute genius in literature. It was funny but up until I started reading his stuff I didn't know men like this existed. I looked up to crooks and famous boxers, I thought all pen-pushers were mugs, they were less than the men I knew.

Tennyson, however made me look at life through a different perspective, he made me realise that some of the things going on in my head were not a form of madness but an acceptance that I had passion, I had loyalty and strong morals. Below are a couple of verse he wrote and the ones that really hit home with me.

Ring out the false, ring in the true.

And out of darkness came the hands that reach thro' nature, moulding men

Knowledge comes, but wisdom lingers.

Guard your roving thoughts with a jealous care, for speech is but the dealer of thoughts, and every fool can plainly read in your words what is the hour of your thoughts.

No man ever got very high by pulling other people down. The intelligent merchant does not knock his competitors. The sensible worker does not knock those who work with him. Don't knock your friends. Don't knock your enemies. Don't knock yourself.

They are just a few of Tennyson's work, the words of a genius! As I read more about him I found myself discovering his soul, he was putting down on paper his wisdom and the words from somewhere very deep. I found myself being in awe of the man, I also found myself believing that I was in some way a kindred spirit of his.

Suddenly everything was opened up for me, the confined ways of my youth were now blown open as I discovered a side to me which had been locked away under years of blindness.

If I am honest it is the short quotes that I truly love, I love long poems but I try not to confine myself to any formula, I believe poetry comes in all guises, in fact I believe poetry cannot be regulated on confined, that is what makes it powerful and special. The ability to be free from any boundaries. Poetry for me is the heart speaking on paper, a thought or passion put into words, it is the finest achievement of mankind in the literary world, better than any novel or epic masterpiece, poetry is natural, it is pure and it is born from passion, whether it great hate or great love, poetry can never be denied.

I feel the blood pump through a broken heart
Yet my will and my thirst for love remain
I am a man...A MAN full of life
Full of passion and full of compassion
I have only one life...I will live it my way
I will feed from my feelings and if I am different...then so be it!
I am free...........FREE!
Joseph Pyle

Poems by
Joseph Pyle SNR

Poetry from the mind of Joseph henry Pyle written when he was in prison
About the author
Joe Pyle is an ex professional boxer turned company director of Touchdown productions film company based at Pinewood. These poems were wriiten in 1996 when he was serving a nine-year prison sentence for a crime which he always maintained his innocence. Joe wrote these selection of poems based on life experience. It is intended as both a gift and a tribute to family and friends who have supported and stood by him throughout.

Farewell

A tribute to Ronnie Kray

The time has come to say my farewell
But there's a few things that I'd like to tell
For twenty-six years they've kept me confined
Saying I'm mad and out of my mind.

I never let my pals down, and I went with the grain
If that's being mad then call me insane
I've done some bad things and I have done good
But good before bad whenever I could

I was deprived of my freedom, for so many years
But I feel no pity or shed no tears
As I'm now free from the screws, and that stinking cell
Free from slop out and that Broadmoor hell

So feel no sadness and please don't mourn
For I haven't disappeared, I am just reborn
And Reg remember, I'm a whisper away
And we'll get it together, again some day

Ode to Ronnie Knight

A few words on Ronnie Knight when they were in HMP Parkhurst together

It's all a ploy as he tenders his garden
Just hoping the governor will give him a pardon
His belly and Cat C are indeed a worry
Hell develop an ulcer, for sure, in a hurry

So Ron 'Give-up!' we've tumbled tour game
It's the isle of Wight, not sunny bloody Spain
Now forget the 'siesta' and clear blue sea
It's the compound in Parkhurst for Jim you and me!

Wilf

A poem for Wilf Pine

When things get tough, Wilf will often say
Do something, follow or get out of the way
When people ask him when 'what' for and why
He tells them to start, with the words ...I'll try!

He sets his aims high, while others may snigger
But he knows the right time to if he needs to pull a trigger
He won't just sit there and 'go by the book'
For you can't climb that mountain, by taking a look

His words...'don't stay where you are, begin where you are'
Go for the jackpot and you'll go far
He's not very fit but he has no fear
Its respect that he has, which we all revere.

Love

To Shirley

Love is a feeling that's hard to explain,
it's something great and sometimes gives pain.
It's a lonely place when love is isn't there,
for our love for each other we have to share.
The bond is so strong now it never shows,

for true love is blind as the story goes.
We will never build walls when our loves at a loss.
but build a bridge for both of us to cross.

You're my queen my wife my friend and my lover,
and the rest of our lives we're spend with each other.
So remember Shirley when we can't see the way.
That when all seems lost our future will stay.

Knowledge

Knowledge can make the wisest man humble
Where ignorant ones are sure to crumble
For a man who know show 'is never at a loss
But the man who thinks why is always his boss

An ignorant man will bear no shame
But when he won't learn, there lies the shame
When you pay for experience, please keep the receipt
For your very own words, you're sure to eat

Experience and knowledge, can never be bought
But what you don't know, you can always be taught
So listen to me and you'll get along
For I'm not always right but I'm never wrong

Youth

Youth is the age where we choose to direct
It's a time of life that we all reflect
But when youth and beauty have faded away
Characters one thing that will always stay

Now elder men argue, and then make laws
then send the youth to fight the wars
if you get into trouble when you're long in the tooth
its quite often blamed on a misspent youth

so look where you're going and not where you've been
for success, not defeat it tomorrows dream
and don't interfere and get in the way
all our future lies in the youth of today

Time

Were gaoled and classed as double 'A'
In a special unit we have to stay
It's a factory of problems one might agree
Where man's only aim is to be set free

A man must be strong and stand up to the screws
For the strong will survive and the weaker will lose
Now one doesn't fail, just by hitting rock bottom
If he doesn't climb back though, he'll soon be forgotten

It's said a good lawyer has plenty of punch
But the clever be sure takes the judge out to lunch
But our freedoms not missed, till it's taken away
The same as the air we breathe every other day

For nobody knows, what the future will tell
Why wait till your thirsty to dig that well?

Achievement

Achievement and fame, can be bought from wealth
But ensure they're not bought at the cost of your health
If the aims are high that you wish to achieve
Then first remember, that you must believe

Your aims won't succeed if you keep asking why
Ones aims are achieved by saying … I'll try!
To have friends and money is easily done
When you've friends and no money, an achievement is won

To achieve one's success, he must be free
And break from the shade, of that ruling tree
So stand firm in your aims, no matter how great
For its choice, not chance, that determines our fate

Action before words

Your guilty if proven you lied at your trial
But the law can lie without denial
Actions make an image we see with our eyes
Spoken louder than words and with fewer lies

Now don't sit back and wait to receive
For actions not words, are ways to achieve
It's from these deeds that men will aspire
As talk is cheap, but the world loves a trier

The one thing you keep when you give is your word
So what is one giving when his promise is heard
Choose what say not say what you choose
As a still tongue and a wise head, don't leave any clues

Unwritten laws

A strong man is one we shouldn't revere
It's the weakness in man that we all should fear
The man who's a genius, we all should admire
But we have no respect for the grass or the liar

We envy the rich man, in his ivory tower
And we fear the man who has plenty of power
A man of the law is supposed to be just
But a man with character is the man that we trust

Be silent and look like a fool to some
Don't open your mouth and talk like one
Look around, stay calm and listen to what's said
For a still tongue will surely, keep a wise head.

The last laugh

When a man can laugh he'll never be poor
If he looks in the mirror and can laugh what he saw
For laughter to life, is like sun to the sea
As they both need each other, and each one is free

If you don't laugh at people, but laugh what they do
Then your brother and sisters will laugh with you
Now a man laughs last, should win the fight
Though it could be a case, of him being polite

A cloak of laughter is used in denials
But the truth will shine through by an honest man's smiles
Let the grin be a warning, coming from a deceiver
While the smile is welcomed when you're the receiver

Conceit

Conceit is god's gift for small minded people
Whose egos are large and minds are feeble
For a man has learned noting when he knows it all
But when riding high he must know how to fall

For a man's who's conceited won't get anywhere
As long as think, he's already there
The head starts to swell, when his mind stops growing
He's a big headed bigot, when his ego starts showing

The conceited man tells what he will do
And the boaster will tell you where and with who
So don't be conceited, walk tall and be proud
Be modest, be humble and don't talk aloud.

Behaviour

behaviour is how one does his deeds
not how he feels and just believes
for its not what you have that makes life worthwhile
it's taking the knocks and wearing a smile

with a staunch friend at hand you'll never be lonely
but a shadow friend shows when the sun shines only
and if a friend wrongs you once then he is to blame
but if he wrongs you twice then you bear the shame

so listen to others opinions too
for the facts may not change but the feelings do
and to keep your friends you must always remember
to bite your lip and not lose your temper

Make your aims high

Face yesterday with no regret
And tomorrow with no worry
Make things easy to start and hard to stop but never in a hurry
Success can be sweet though the secret is sweat
And you can't each your heights by just casting your net

So know what you want and do what it takes
And remember to lift, your foot off the brakes
As success always comes from love, not hate
Nor luck or a fluke as failure will state

Make your success a lifelong quest
But one never fails if he tries his best
For the failure of others make sure you get wise
Then you won't change your hat, for a larger size.

Freedom

The fight for freedom has gone on for years
As laws to oppose it, are held by our peers
The freedom of man is set out in print
But a man's only free when he's proven skint

We will never have freedom while people suffer
For freedoms not gained by ruling another
That men are born free was gods intent
So why govern others without their consent

If freedom is taken, don't relent on your views
For the freedom of mind, a man cannot lose
Now the highway of freedom is the route from hate
But the roles will reverse if you sit back and wait

My Son

Joe, I haven't been there to guide you along
So here's a few words to keep you from wrong
As you go through life, stand tall and be proud
Choose your words first and don't think aloud

Be bold in what you stand for
But be careful in what you fall for
Keeps your morals and principles well in your sight
And know your wrongs as well as your rights

And before you criticise another
Look carefully at your sister's brother
A little man may criticise
It takes a big man with heart to sympathise

There goes nothing

I've been through much in this life that I have lived
Through good times and bad times but I've never hid
Men don't shed tears they just brood and sigh
But there's tears in the heart that don't reach the eye
A man is not rich by possessions alone
But by our values and not what we own

I have a great family and I couldn't want more
If I never get fortunes, I'll never be poor
In my search for riches I've sometimes aimed high
But I can't lose these things that money can't buy

They've put me away for breaking the law
But my crime in life was being born poor
So to live in this world but once is tough
But to live it fast then once is enough

The other man's grass

Some people kneel and pray for rain
But when they get mud they start to complain
We have to be grateful for what we have got
And show no regret for what we have not

To a man who has money, friends easily come
But friends when he's broke he can count on his thumb
So remember that life will pass you by fast
For a man's not so rich he can buy back his past

Money

Fools make money and money makes fools
And a fool with money, will break all the rules
When a poor man complains, it's for what he has not
When a rich man complains, he wants the lot
Now money can't buy you a friend who is true
For that kind of friend could be bought from you

Make money your servant and not your master
If you don't, you'll go bankrupt a whole lot faster
Now gambling's an illness, some would say
So the dice are thrown best, when you throw them away

Cast the first stone

When you know what is right, but you don't see it through
Your still doing wrong in the judge's view
When one judge's others he should be fair
But an unbiased judge, is indeed very rare

If your judging one's future, don't look at the past
When you judge what is gone, the future won't last
So if you're making judgment, one shouldn't condemn
For you could be wrong as we'll as them

We all have a right to give our opinion
But we don't have a right to expect them to listen
So don't sit in judgment on other men's deeds
Till you've walked where they've walked and know all their needs

Argumentive

Arguments have three sides, but ones out of sight
There's your side, their side and the side that's right
When one is wrong he should never argue
But one is right, he should never need to

When one makes you angry, he conquers you too
So always keep cool when one argues with you

The cure for anger, it's said is delay
To make peace and make up, the following day
And if you argue with fools and cannot tell
Its odds on they think, you're a fool as well

Words of Wisdom

Have courage and nerve, but take heed 'fore' you speak
Learn the wisdom to listen with tongue still in cheek
People only believe, what they see today
So don't try to fool them, with what you say

The words 'I Promise' do not mean enough
For works, not words, are the proof of love
The one thing you keep, when you give, is your word!
So it's better to act, than just be heard

Now failure, can make an honest man lie
But remember the worst thing, is not to try
Some think the answer, to all is money
But many a bee, has drowned in his honey

Poems by
Joseph Pyle Jnr

Joe Pyle Jnr & Joe Pyle Snr
Pic. Credit; Jocylyn Bain Hogg

Stench of betrayal

There is nothing so wretched as a man who betrays
Looks in my eyes and sees only what it pays
A shallow man is disgraceful to himself and his kin
Life's not about, all you can win
Don't drag me down, into your hole
I'm a man of grace, a man of soul
I don't bow with pressure nor ask the cost
For to do that just once, then all is lost
I stand in the trench and won't leave your side
Nothing more precious than my children's pride
Life is hard and we fight every day
When a friend gives his favour, we shouldn't look for pay
to be a man in this world, you have to be strong
stay true to your word and you cannot be wrong
there is always a finish but also a start
yet you can't reach the finish if you don't have heart
so if you have no soul, then stay away from me
cos your betrayal will surface, I will surely see

The Path

By Joe Pyle Jnr

Every now and then we come to a crossroads in our life, a time of great contemplation where we must choose a path to proceed. Do we stay on the path we know? The path that has become tiresome and predictable, or do we take the unknown path?

Do we rid ourselves from the baggage of life, the same weight that has now become almost unbearable to carry and seek out new ideas and new challenges, or stay the same?

Stay on the same familiar path that we have walked upon for most of our lives; continue into old age walking safely upon ground already trodden.

Life can play funny games with you, you may already be frightened for what lays ahead, worse you may be dreading what lies ahead, yet still we continue to walk hand in hand with familiarity, and still we repeat what we did yesterday.

Amongst all this fear time passes by, another day, another month, another year. Slowly it takes pieces away from you, as we grow old we begin to lose those who we love, we lose our parents and those who we once called close friends disappear as our paths drift apart. Our health and vitality drift away, the energy we once had slowly ebbs into decisiveness, we question if we have the time left to complete what we once dreamt of.

Every morning before our eyes we see our face another day older, our dreams another day lost.

Every day the unknown path feels more frightening, the heart says yes and the mind says no!

Personally, I thrive on new challenges, I need them or I feel like I am dying. It is the unknown that brings me to life; it fills me with youthful optimism and inspires the soul of a poet in me.

So just do it! Just go for it!

If your life has come to a standstill and you ache for new adventures, then throw off your confines and take the new path.

Whatever happens, you would have added to your experience of life and if it doesn't work out then all you have lost is endless familiarity and a dreary race to your grave.

I want to Live

I want to fly...
No longer will I sit in darkness and hide among these walls
I want to unleash the life within, bring the world into my life.
Grasp life by the throat and squeeze what I want.
Rid myself of the fears and negativities and fly on the hopes of freedom and beauty.
No longer will I fear what will happen.
Grasp this life and fly with hope in my heart, enthusiasm and joy as I look at the sunshine through eyes of optimism.
No more hiding in the shadows, scared that I may make a mistake.
To hell with them...I will live!
Live as a free man...live as a human being, full of love and passion.
I will throw off my chains, rise from the confines of pressure and doom.
I have one life and I will live it.
My will and zest must break free, now is the time, no more waiting.
Fly...fly... and find my worth, it is there ... buried in chains of baggage.
Buried by those who fear me being so free.
I want glens and meadows of sunshine, the feel of a warm breeze on my brow and the feeling of satisfaction that when my time is finally over I can say I did everything I could to live my life to its full.
Today I rise from a huddled position, frightened to be seen...today I stand and open my arms and smile as I smell the world...today I embrace life...today I begin to live.

Wrath

Blow your battle horns and stoke your fires,
A dawn of vengeance is coming,
A time of change is approaching like a tsunami crashing against the land,
I smell the fear in you and feel your confusion,
You have made me,
You have created your own doom,
There is no stopping me now; I come for you and your life.
Everything you knew will now come crashing down,
You pushed too far, you laughed too much,
I was content to live, but you were not content to leave me alone.
Now I come for you with all of my power,
The power of one who can take no more,
A lifetime of constriction will soon be released upon you,
It will be like a volcano as I explode my anger upon you,
You cannot defend such angst,
You are now on the precipice of destruction,
You have sowed the seed of your own oblivion.

A Friend in need is a Friend indeed

What is a man when he has won and lost?
A man who is staunch ..., no matter the cost.
A man who is strong, a man who is fair
A man who can love, a man who can care,
To be a friend, to be a mate
When you are in trouble I'll never be late,
A man you can trust, I am your friend
Behind your back, I'll always defend,
I'm always here and have your back
When you are wrong I will pull you back on track,
Advice I give will always be true
For it is only suggested for the love I have in you,
I'm a man of the past, a relic of time
I am what I am, no matter the crime,
I'll be here for you no matter the test
Cos the morals I have are simply the best,
Don't judge my life, judge how I live
Ignore all the rumours and see how I give,
I'm just a man, made from simple flesh and bone
But my ways and my soul are mine to own,
To be my friend you have nothing to fear
Because when trouble comes your way, you know I'll be near,
I won't run away, I won't look to hide
I have too much loyalty too much pride,
So, you be the judge and you decide
Do you want me with you and by your side,
Cos when the bullets fly and others run
I'll be the one pulling a gun.

Its … On!

I cannot eat, I cannot sleep
Don't have time to sigh and weep
They're coming for me, they are on their way
This is my life, just another day
They told me there are armed, they carry a gun
Bullets are gonna fly, back at you my son
You think I am afraid, you try to scare
You picked the wrong man, I just don't care
Drive by shooting! Spray your burst
You better prey and beg I don't see you first
So, we're going to war, we're going all the way
It's my turn now, you have had your say
You called me on the phone and said I am dead
As soon as you see me, I'm getting one in the head
So now you're committed, you must carry out your threat
But believe me you fool, you shouldn't have taken this debt
If you think I'll back down, you're in for a shock
I come from staunch, solid, unafraid stock
You're now in the big league, there's no turning back
If I were you, I'd hit the road jack
You have given me no option, pushed me against a wall
Now all I can do is fight and stand tall
If you're gonna kill me, then you're getting it first
Rather than die, I'd rather be cursed.

My Sons

Stand tall, walk proud
Never too brash or never too loud
Lead from the front, lead as you live
Be wary how you take and wise when you give
Protect your honour and stand by what you trust
Even if it means returning to dust
Watch your words closely, never barter with talk
It is stronger to listen than join the walk
Be vigilant to lies, see through their verses
Judgement is silence than deal in curses
Silently study the ways of the weak
Then trust in you view and let your heart speak
Never be prudish, be open to all
Yet know the decision is yours to call
Be confident in your body, be solid, but care
The greatest of men is the one who is fair
If you are challenged with uncertainty, then take a retreat
It is better to think than rush to defeat
Remember my son to use your head wise
Never be bitter never show despise
Compassion and empathy are what makes you strong
Helping first will never make you wrong
Live your life free and don't hang your head in shame
You have a duty to your children who will carry your name
When all seems lost, you must reach within
Sometimes it will be hard when it's easier to sin
But remember your background, and who you are
Know that my love will never be far
You will soon be a man with the world as your stage
So live it free and not in a cage
The worst kind of prison is the one in your mind
Walk past your fears and never look behind

It is your life to live so you live it free
Be yourself for all to see
The most precious of gifts is my advice to be true
But it is your life my son and yours to do.....

Sonny Joe, Cassius and Manny

Rouse Yourself

Rouse yourself
As did the former lions of your blood
Discover the grit that belonged to your grandfather
Furry the brow and breathe a deep
Clench your teeth as you stiffen with pride
All that you wish is yours to take
You are my king, their king
The king of the world
Let no man utter indifference
Before you I kneel as others do wish
For you my liege we will shake the heavens
Do not hither with time
For the time of your merit has surely arrived.
Let those who scorn, now shake in fear
Let those who conspire, be fearful of the night
Rouse yourself, my majestic of majesties
Rouse your lions and unleash your kingdom
The time for destruction has come
The time of your wraith sits impatient at the door
Let those who scoff, cower in fear
Let those who oppose be driven to dust
Now my liege, the legacy of your ancestor's rests in your regal hands
Make them proud, take back what was theirs
And in doing so send the starkest of messages
Let no other king sit on his throne unless allegiance is offered.
Rouse yourself my liege
Rouse this nation that stands before you
On bended knee, I beg of thee
Let all and sunder see your mightiness.

Locked away

When you imprison a man, you free his spirit
You lock his body away behind a wall
But you create a feeling with so much more power
Nothing is as strong as a man wanting to be free
You create a resolute hatred of what you do
This man will detest you...he will do whatever it takes to free his body
Even if freedom is gained by death
You lock a man away; you lock away yourself.
The time has come for us to look at who we are.
Are our children to be slaves like us or will they live their lives as free men
and women.
The decision is 'ours,' gentlemen.
Either we act or we crawl back under the rock we have been living under for
far too long.

The Eagle

The eagle flies high above their heads
Below him are the ravens and crows
As time goes by the eagle befriend the birds flying below him.
He flies above them every day and they are of help to him as they show him
where to find food
As the eagle swoops he captures his prey and shares what is left with the
crows
At first all is well until the crows start to wish they were eagles
They bicker and become resentful; they pretend they are friends with the
eagle just so they can take what they can.
Soon the eagle begins to see their betrayal, he is too wise not to,
Below him the crows are scheming and trying to find ways to copy the eagle
But the eagle just looks, he laughs to himself as he knows he doesn't need
them.
He befriended them because he wanted to, not because he needed them.
The eagle then tries to remind the crows that they are just crows, he
swoops above their heads at blistering speed where he shows them his
magnificence, he even captures another prey and allows them the fruit of
his deed, just in the hope they can remain friends.
But there is no stopping the crows now, they are full of envy and greed,
they are no longer interested in friendship, all they want is to be, is the
eagle.
The eagle has two choices; does he swoop and attack the crows that have
grown fat from his labour and show them that can never be what he is?
Again, the eagle is too wise for this, why should he attack and risk injury,
why should he lower himself to attack the crows who exist in the sky below
him.
The eagle needs no one, he will just fly away and find somewhere else to
feed and in doing so he sends a stark message to the crows……
You are all just crows, and that is all you will ever be.

Breaking Bread

I don't know if you know how the world works?

Maybe you know how your world works, but let you tell me how my world works.

Firstly, you come into my company and we break bread, from that crust I let you break bread with a contact of mine. Then behind my back you put your knife into another loaf.

Together you take a bite, together you share the bread behind my back ... now not one of you think, maybe Joe would like a piece of bread. We are both here at this table because of Joe, should Joe not be privileged of this meeting?

Now let me tell you about my world... I live in a world where I trust my friends, when I break bread between us I expect us to share. I don't expect to share my loaf between two friends only for them to meet another day and hide their bread from me.

Is that the action of a friend, or is that the action of someone who cares not for my friendship?

Now in my world if someone is taking from my table and then not sharing from theirs then such an action provokes a response. How should I react to someone who feeds from my goodwill only to hide in the shadows and betray my kindness?

What action should I take? Shall I let that man redeem his action, or should I condemn that man without retribution, should I take him into my world and give him the flip side of my friendship....

The coward

I will do everything in my power to ruin and scold your deed
There will be books written of your cowardice, scholars will speak your
name in lowered voice
Men will scorn you till the end of time; men will lay shame at your blood
There will be no grave for your bodies to lie
No words said over your dead bodies
Just scorn and hatred, an eternity of detestation
Revulsion, dishonour, infamy and abhorrence
That is your reward for this wicked deed on this day.
Take these forth and dispose them to their fate
Shame, eternal shame.

Poor

When you have lots of money, all seems fine
Everything's gravy and fine cultured wine
You walk with cockiness, speak fast and brash
Gloating around with pockets full of cash
But something is lost; you take your eye off the ball
Ignorant your next step could end in a fall
Blinded by conceit, you lose your will
Walking on air, forsaking your skill
Flash cars and suits but something's amiss
Ambition fades as you walk in the midst
Am I still free, is this what I choose
I'm much more alive when I have nothing to lose.

Cannot Stop me

Cannot stop me, cannot piss on my spirit
Never, no matter what I keep moving forward,
Sometimes it's like I am running a race in concrete boots
Every step kills, every step rips my flesh from the bone,
But I grow more fucking flesh, I never tire, I never give up
I will move forward, I will overcome all your fucking obstacles,'
Shoot me, stab me, slander me, try whatever you fucking like
With every fucking act of betrayal, I will haunt you more,
With every barrier, you push at me
I grow stronger and more determined,
I never stop coming forward, I will never be beaten
Even in my grave I will haunt your memories,
Even in death I will cast a shadow on your life
I will embarrass you, make you question your merit,
Destroy you from your own actions; you will burn in my glory
Combust in my wrath, cower from my reputation,
A man is a fucking man in any world
I am just me and that is a man, a man of feeling and principle,
When you are dead and gone, you are buried in history
When I am dead and gone, I am revered in history,
People don't remember money they remember principle
They remember a man who lived and died for what he believed in,
They remember someone they know they can trust; someone they know
they can rely on.
Do whatever you fucking want
I have already seen it, planned for it and pissed on it,
Whatever happens I keep moving forward.
I never stop, never, forget fucking flesh and bone
I live by my spirit, live by my heart.

Passion

Everybody's hero! When I am gone, they will remember me
They will remember the way I lived and the way that I gived.
NEVER again will I ask for help, never again will I bend on one knee and swallow my pride
I am what I am, full of fucking passion and full of life
To turn your back on me is to turn your back on truth
Never again will you find that truth
A man willing to die for you, willing to go where others will not go
But I will remember and I will use it to once again fly to the heavens
I will crush all before me with glory
Men will curse themselves every morning of their lives that they let such devotion walk away
I am what I am and that is truth!
I am real, truth and something which only comes from the soul
I pledge this passion that I will once again burst from the flames and rise in splendour
Forsaken but still proud,
Only fools cannot see such worth.
Do you fucking know how much pain it caused me to bend on one knee?
Can you fucking contemplate how embarrassing that was?
I knelt with a hand of friendship, then rose with a look of despise
I slowly rose and hid the tears and then took a solemn vow make you so regret your decision.
Now it is my addiction, my journey to break your fucking hearts
To turn your back on me cannot hurt me, it cannot destroy me
What it does is show me your value of me
And be rest assured I am coming for you, be assured I will show you the errors of your ways
I will break every sinew and vessel in my body to crush your foolishness
I would kill for you! ... What is the flip side of that? What is the flip side of such passion?
Please joke, please mock! Please shrug your shoulders, please pay no attention.
I want you not expectant; I want you not valuing me, for you are not my friend

You chose not to be and now a wrath more powerful than anything you have seen is unleashed
I am the proprietor of your fucking doom.
Enjoy what you have and I don't give a fuck about giving you fair warning
Because by turning your back on me you have set into motion a chain of events which nothing can stop.

The Law

The laws of this once great land were written quiet in vain
For there are certain individuals who fail to follow the grain.
The pitfall is punishment if captured committing a crime
The burglar, the blagger, they're gonna get some time.
But if a copper does a crime and is unlucky he is caught
Then why are there no charges on him, are ever brought.
Scotland yard's a joke .... They're rotten to the core
A haven for bent coppers, well above the law.
How many more times are we gonna hear a case
Coppers telling lies, corruption on their face.
We all know of their reluctance to bring their own up on a charge
Just internal reprimanding, bent copper still at large.
So, if you wish to be a villain you should become a copper
For they're the bastards with a license
to do it good and proper.

Life is too short

Life is too short to pretend
I live in a life where I mix with street and politicians
I am what I fucking am, just me,
No pretend, no trying to be something I am not
Just a man, a friend and a man who lives with no bosses
I trust my heart, live by it, trust it,
No matter what, I will not change
No matter what comes my way I am what I am,
 I wear my heart on my sleeve, I can't help that, I live life,
Life doesn't live me,
I breathe freedom,
I cannot be someone else,
I look in the mirror and see me,
 I see someone who embraces the romance of being
Injured, cut, bruised,
Yet still the same, nothing can alter that
My kin lived for me to be me
For me to be just a man,
Just a man who wants to live life pure
No fucking betrayals, no fucking back stabbing
I am too proud for that, too bound by my honour
Take it or leave it, I am me,
Just a man... a man who lives by my heart.

Nothing to Lose

When you have lots of money, all seems fine
Everything's gravy and fine cultured wine
You walk with a cockiness, speak fast and brash
Gloating around with pockets full of cash
But something is lost, you take your eye off the ball
Ignorant your next step could end in a fall
Blinded by conceit, you lose your will
Walking on air, forsaking your skill
Flash cars and suits but something's amiss
Ambition fades as you walk in the midst
Am I still free, is this what I choose
I'm much more alive when I have nothing to lose.

Ode to the Somme

The sun has set and now the horror of the night begins
I look around in our trench, our trench filled of mud and blood
besides me stand the men who I call brothers
We live together, fight together, die together
Last night we lost Martin... a bullet just below the eye
Silence then the terrifying sound of a sniper's rifle
We duck down and then next to us we hear the thud
The thud of a brother
Life gone in an instant.
We turn with mixed emotion, for a brief moment we thank god it wasn't us
Then the horror hits home, the horror of another good man, another
brother lost to this soulless war.
Maybe tonight a sniper's bullet will seek me
Maybe tonight it will seek the brother standing next to me
We question our sanity every moment of every day
One moment we hope it will be us next, the next moment we prey we will
make it home to our families.
Tonight, I will look to avenge my brother, again just like the night before.
Looking out into the darkness, waiting for another sniper's bullet
This is the reality of where we are, we cannot see where the shots are
coming from
We only know they will come.
A whistle blows in the distance; we look at each other knowing that many
men will fall
Advance! The sergeant screams, advance! As the sound of the Gatling gun
fills our souls.
If I ever make it out of this hell hole, that sound of death, the Gatling gun
will forever ring in my ears.
I stand hear wet, cold, terrified but I grit my teeth for Britain!

I am a British man through and through and this is my duty

If tonight it is my turn to fall, then let my family know that their father, son and brother has fallen for the empire.

I have met my maker with a Lee-Enfield in my hand and a heart full of pride that I was here fighting for what I believe.

The mud is up to my knees as a rat scrambles past me, six months ago, I would have jumped in the air, now I just smile as they walk amongst us

The horrors of this trench are truly unimaginable, yet there is now nowhere I would rather be,

Besides my brothers, dressed in the uniform of my King, fighting the fight of the righteous.

If I die tonight, then maybe I have merited that right

Let me take that bullet rather than it let it strike my brother

For god, the king and my empire

But most of all, for the man who shares this hell besides me.

King or Fool

I created my demons, I cast the mold
Lived with a heart, soulless and cold
The life of a villain, a life of pretend
Couldn't care less whose life I would end
I sat at the top and destroyed those I knew
Never trusted anyone ... spoke only to few
The blood on my hands was not from my skin
The tears on my cheek were not for my kin
To some I was terror, to some I was god
Ruling my manor with a cruel iron rod
I robbed for money, stole from whoever
Take-take-take was my only endeavour
But what did I win? What glory can I claim?
Scars on faces and hands that maim
Standing in pubs, suited to the nines
Any late payments I dished them all fines
Stoic, hard, dealing in pain
Crushing the feelings of those in vain
But now I am older, repentant and wise
But I look at life with tear glazed eyes.

Blood-Stained Throne

I've seen men who should be patient acting in haste
I've seen a man stick a blade down another man's face
Sometimes I wonder on our crazy race
I've seen lots of rip-offs' experienced the cons
Wondered of the winners and what they have won
I've tried to decipher what life's all about
But always my conclusion is an anger to shout
It seems we are living a life full of lies
One that doesn't care if our brother dies
One, which is stained by the filthy hand of wealth
One where we joke at another's ill health
It seems now we all know too much for our own good
Once upon a time men knew where they stood
Now we all want which have only the few
An idiom in life which is hardly new
But once we were destined from our place of birth
With our family and friends, we all knew our worth
We accepted our lives and got on with living
We all helped our own and lived our lives giving
But now born a man filled with anger in his breed
Caring for himself is his only need
The tools he embraces are jealousy and pain
He is ruthless, cunning, greedy and vain
He wants to succeed in a world of success
He will tread upon anyone as he strives to be best
What is a man when he stands alone?
Arrogantly sitting on his blood-stained throne
So insecure in his make believe life
Boosting his ego giving other men strife
Choking on the fumes of the power he needs
Ruining lives as his pocket he feeds
Wearing his crown pretending that he's king
Constantly dreaming of what more wealth will bring
Live all your life hurting your brothers

Paying no regard to the feelings of others
You think your superior because you have money
But to those who can see, your wit is not funny
But one day like us you're going to die
Then you'll answer to god for living your lie
But then it's too late, there is no return
The price of your wealth is a destiny to burn!

Bested but not Beaten

Shackled to a chair gasping for air
Blood on the floor waiting for more
Now all alone I am hurt to the bone
Yet inside I smile
Day after day they have tortured my body
Still I am strong I have given them nobody
Cut with a knife and beaten with a stick
Russian roulette as I hear another click
Haven't seen the sun for days on end
Yet its warmth shines brightly as my honour I defend
Tell me the names of the men you protect
Punch after punch only strengthens my reject
Yesterday I was close, close to confess
Today I am past the limit, I couldn't care less
You have played your hand and given me your best
I have now come through your barbaric test
You didn't break me on the first day, now your methods have failed
The more you hit me just makes me more proud
I won't give you anything, only my scorn
Any hope you had is now forlorn
Take off my blindfold; let me see your eyes
I can taste your frustration as yourself respect dies
Hit me, strike me, let me feel another blow
But your never force me to tell you all I know
I am willing to die and go to my grave
With a smile on my face knowing friend's I have saved
Let them live long and let them be free
Let them remember the friend in me
I will rise into heaven with my soul complete
You have taken my life but yours is defeat
Open your arms to me Jesus my lord
I went out fighting holding my sword
So, who has won and who has lost

You can have my life but at what cost
You tried everything you knew to make me talk
Now get out of my way and let me walk
You're a coward, a rat, a man full of doubt
Look at me now as pride I shout
Just walk out the door and leave me alone
I am stronger than you though you've bled me to the bone
Doesn't matter anymore, anything you do
I'm willing to die as long as I'm true
You smashed me near death now you know your mistake
Two men in a room, only one man is fake
I've took your blows and took your threats
And all that you have done is learned regret
The only thing left is you'll hear me rejoice
Defiance and pride are filling my voice
I see your anger I smell your hate
But I'd rather die true than have your fate
I have won, you have lost
Now walk away and remember the cost...

What I am

My determination shall neither writher nor bend
Instead it shall draw strength from your mocks
Resulting in absolute success, so I invite your jestful remarks
For their spoken word inspires me to spit back those conceited and
Foolish words that were once uttered to me
For I am a man who dances with ambition and those who once mocked me
with doubts to inflate their own egos and importance shall one day
Scream with grief and rue the day that they spoke so selfishly to me
As I grow older and my power grows, I shall remember my friends and
Equally my foes and my justice shall be wielded on both
The man who crosses my path shall meet with only two fates
Joy or pain with each gift given to their extremes
My hands carry sin and my heart carries grief and my body carries
Neglect and abuse
Scar tissue in abundance with every scar bearing its own painful tale
But my head carries hope and determination, passion and romance and a
Strength that shall take me to the forever-ness of .... the stars.

To stand and not crawl

I feel the blood pump through a broken heart
Yet my will and my thirst for love still remain
I am a man...A MAN full of life
Full of passion and full of compassion
I have only one life...I will live it my way
I will feed from my feelings and if I am different...then so be it
I am free............FREE!

Integrity

To go against everything that you know
And not be afraid of fear to show
To refuse what is good for you and accept which is bad
When all common sense is calling you mad
To reach deep within and grasp which is right
To stand up and be counted though no solution is in sight
To stick by your honour when you know it means pain
To show perseverance when they call you insane
To feel content when you're cast out alone
No one's as lonely as a king lost his throne
To start at the beginning when your achievements went far
And hide the secret that your soul is so scarred
To lose everything that you have ever known
Be proud of your nakedness, honour flesh and bone
Your flesh may be bound but your soul remains free
It's how deep you look as to how far you see.

Father

I see my father when I look at my reflection
I see his smile, I see his eyes
As a tear falls I see his love
As my brow furrows I feel his compassion
I swallow deep and think of things I never said
My lip trembles and I sense his soul
He lives in me and in my sons
Every day if I look hard he is with me
In my blood - in my bones
In my heart and in my dreams
How I miss the pat on the head,
The hand on my hand
And the occasional embrace
If I try hard I can hear his voice
It is my voice now
His mind Is my mind
Just one more smile father
Just one more tear
I am your son and all your hopes
Now you are gone - I am no longer the son
I am the father now.

Pressure

When you live on the other side of the fence, everything is magnified by the hundreds, you hear people say about pressure and I wonder if some people have actually looked up the meaning of the word. You hear stories like Nick Leeson was under pressure, please! Robbing millions and millions of pounds, yeah right pressure! That to me is like winning the lottery, I would be having the time of my life.

Then we see that the England football manager is under intense pressure, of course he is! It must be driving him mad wondering where and what to spend his six million pound wages on.

To us pressure is fighting for your fucking life!

Pressure is when you have to move out your family and go to war because someone is coming to do war with you.

Pressure is about making the right decision, a decision squeezed between going to prison for life or catching a bullet in the fucking eye.

Our life is glamorous but so it should be as there are not many who can survive it, pressure is about trying to get out of something all your life when you know it is the one thing you are best at.

They say live by the sword and die by the sword, that is a great saying but to us it's a fucking stark warning, almost a premonition, a reality we strive daily to avoid. Now that's fucking pressure.

Sorry but I must Go …

I am leaving
So sad but I have to go
I am ripped apart here. you have stabbed me in the heart too many times
I must take flight and fly away to ventures new
I will take what I have and live my life
You have taken enough of my energy…. taken enough of my life
Tore the flesh from my soul
Made me question my sanity…made me question my integrity
Only when I am gone will you realise your actions
Only when you fall and you see there is no one to pick you up again
And if there is what toll will they ask
I gave for nothing
I was yours, your rock, your crutch…the one you could rely on
Now that's gone…you betrayed yourself
Goodbye my friend…I forgive you. and I will cherish the moments we had
But I am sorry I am too full of passion to be used anymore
I took so much pain…so much agony…dreaming of something that never existed
I am leaving…. I have to go
 I am too alive to stay.

Constrained

The concrete castle of your mind
confined, restricted, utterly blind
you fester and fidget, you scheme and plot
constantly cursing of what you have not
fuelled with bile, jealousy and greed
fooled into believing its vengeance you need
you
constantly worrying what others are feeling
tales of success send you reeling
totally driven with envy and spite
you've forgotten reality, forgot what's right
choosing to live in the shadows of others
hating success from the sons of mothers
angered, enraged, full of hate
why have you forgot, you have your own fate
your up-tight and squeezed, bound in barbed wire
eyes of greed burning with fire
Tin pot Hitler, cursed in your own dream
bitter and twisted, planning your scheme
your mind has trapped you, imprisoned your heart
but you must break free, find where to start
only you can break yourself free
only you can accept it is me
forget what's expected and live life true
you're limping through life with only one shoe
try to relax and just have some fun
rid this angst of what others have won

Had Enough

I will tear this pain away
I refuse to be confined by it anymore
Like the phoenix, I shall rise from this den of lies
I will rise from within
I will stand erect and spit my defiance as I use it to move on
No more. No more can I be involved
No more can I be used
No more can I have my heart broken
No more.... can I fool myself
You have taken your pound of flesh
Cashed in your 30 coins of silver
My life is now my own...from your deceit you have given me freedom
I AM free...free from the burdens you placed on me
Free to live once again
Free to be myself
Free to embrace my life again
FREE to breathe...free to exist.

Twas the day

Twas a day where fate appeared
In the midst, I could feel this was the day where my name would be born
If I live or die, today I will be membered
God give me the strength to be just
Guide my heart to truthfulness
Do not let temptation divert my worth
Let me be strong, for those who follow will have to live with my actions
Those who I face I face without feeling
Only what I must do, not what I want to do
Today is the day I am willing to die
Please god let it be for the common good
If I am a fool, then make my death come swift
If I carry your word, then guide my will for your salvation
Only truth and justice can I be strong
Only from sufferance can my legacy be revered
Today I give you all I am
Today I stand tall or fall proud
Make my life worthy of your teaching
Make my day, a day of pride
For when all is forgotten and all are long gone
It is truth that shall live through all eternity.

The Critic

He prowls on the keyboard waiting to pounce
Your hard-earned work he is going to trounce
He will tear you shreds ruin your page
He is big-headed and bitter, the computer his stage
Doesn't care if he injures or care who he hurts
His swansong in life is dishing the dirt
Too self-interested to worry about others
Sons, daughters, fathers and mothers
What kind of person wants to belittle?
Must be a person whose life is so brittle
He believes he's superior, oh what a fool
Harming others is not very cool
Don't you realise how much pain you cause
Is there nothing between your ears that makes you pause?
Why do you do it?
What good does it achieve?
Do you think you are clever, is that what you believe?
Are you a person; is there a beat in your chest?
Tearing at feelings, is that your best?
I can't understand, your life must be so sad
What insecurities makes you so bad?
Maybe I am crazy and put faith in all men
Only to be disappointed again and again
The reviewer on amazon, a home of the bitter
As bad as the trolls on youtube and twitter
Do you feel better now you've had your say
You feel all important as you ruin someone's day
So well done, hope you feel proud
Had your rant and done it so loud
But remember this saying and remember it well
Remember it when your head starts to swell
A little man may criticize
It takes a man with a big heart to sympathise.

The Heart as One

The language of the heart
How is it understood, so many times it falls on deaf ears?
So many times, it is just walked on by
Take the time to listen...take the time to feel
Listen...don't just hear
See the pain in my eyes and see my actions
Inside I am pleading, begging for you to understand
I want you to live...I want you to feel the passion
Embrace it...fall in love with it...live your life with it
I am dying inside, being this alone
As one we are unbeatable
But only when we look at each other with the language of the heart.

A Friend

Did they expect us to show them respect?
Prove your worth first
Show your friendship
Earn my love
Then…… Just then you will have the best friend in the world
I will stand by you with my life
Even when you stab me in the back I will value my side of what we had
You cannot even see that when you hurt me you injure yourself
If you can't see what a friend you have in me, then was my affection wasted
I give you everything I have and you return lies
You destroy your soul when you try to outwit me
I see you…I see everything you do…my silence, as I pray that I am wrong
only fuels your betrayal
Maybe one day you will realise your betrayal
But because I was your friend and I loved you, I pray you never do
Now I must say goodbye, farewell and good luck
I can no longer live amongst the lies and the festering stench of betrayal
I will just go my own way….
Again, on my own.

Be a Man

To always stay composed and never lose your head
To keep you're cool even in the hottest situations
Never deal in threats, play your cards close to your chest
Children use threats as toys of their egos
To always imagine what the other man is thinking thus you
Remain one step ahead
Take heed to caution but do not let it be your master
Caution can be your enemy as well as your friend
Family business must remain within
Never use it as a tool of gossip
To always be fair but don't let fairness make you humble
Twist your threats so the listener hears advice
Anger and rashness decays what they set out to achieve
Nothing is settled by anger, and the man you impose it upon
Will only one day seek his revenge?
To always help the needed though only if just
Keep your eyes open to those who need your help most
A true friend will seldom ask for it
To never seek to disgrace or belittle a man
Your own self-esteem will be the most injured
To remember that true wisdom holds the art of reasoning
Animals in the jungle don't reason, kings, leaders and wise men do
Learn how to master this art for it shall never do you harm if used
Sincerely
Never let drink get the better of you, it will only harm outlooks against you
and one day you may have to answer for it
Know when to say no though never be prudish or patronising
Never judge anyone by your own standards or look down on them because
they do not possess the virtues that have moulded you a man
Never deal in lies, to lie to a man means to look up to him or pity yourself
Be proud in yourself and be strong in your mind
Do not throw apologies around too often, a truly sorry man does not need
to apologise
Though always look out for the exception, accidents do happen.

In This Dark Age

This sick world where smiles hide conceit
Where I matter more than you
Where what I possess is the scale that is used to judge
Where sex is no longer privacy
Where it is chic in social get together's to speak of the unspeakable in order
to shock ....why ....who wants to shock!
Bombarded daily by impossible goals, inferiority complexes are rampant
Friends give advice just to boost their self-egos
Politicians lie........... What's new....... Blatant, carelessness, ignorance, and
nonchalance
Robbing the robbed when will it stop
The age of idleness, no one wants to try for fear it won't work .... What
arrogance, what insanity
Everyone's a genius, everyone's a teacher,
Everyone's a star, everyone's a scholar, everyone's a movie star,
How naive you all are
How you build walls around the lives you live
Prisoners of the 90's
The rich, the handsome and athletic is held above the poor the sick and
disabled
How shallow you all are
Admiration has evolved into obsession! Crazy!
What sick twisted society evolved from Thatcher and TV
Ignoring family traditions and beliefs and accept the words of some Yankee
actor on TV .... What a terrible disgrace you must be in the eyes of your
father
But you don't care.......... Caring's in the past, caring's for the weak, the
weak are outcasts ....why! .... Why!
Some people are born weak it was a card dealt to them by nature, so how
can you criticise these people, what monsters are you if you do
God has been forsaken, who needs god when we have Hollywood!
Respect! .... what's that I hear you say!
Hidden faces everywhere .... Shrouded in masks of fear
What a travesty it is that we cannot show our real self's

Why can't we give our love without conditions?
Stick a needle in your arm and hide for a while ... Ah it feels good .... You fool!
Destroy the life that your parents created, that's respect
Selfishness! Greed! I, is all you disgustingly think
Some of you out there are good but not enough
Oh, not enough ....oh not enough
Mothers no longer teach their children about god
A little girl robbed from the beauty of faith .... What kind of mothers are you?
I have more than you........ O' you lucky people! One day as time flies by your metal will rust your house will fall and your clothes will rot but what of you spirit what of your soul
Did your flash cars, flash houses, and fancy clothes really matter?
Richness is the soul and not the hand when will you all remember again
Has it all gone too far, is it all too late
Where has the gentleman, society gone, the one which we all adored
Has women's lib destroyed it
Oh, what a terrible shame if such nobility has been lost!

True to my Word

Well, I've had a good run
I've had some great and glorious times
I've seen sights you could not begin to believe
I've felt passion that is eternal
Felt feelings only Gods could feel
It's been my life
I've lived my way without boundaries or your laws
I've felt love few could comprehend
Pride which fills your lives with envy
Money you've only dreamed of
Power that would chill your beliefs
Respect that you sadly never understood
I am a man true to my word .... True to my honour .... True to myself
and the ways of my ancestry
You live your life sheltering under the blanket of cowardice and betrayal
You walk in the shadows for you are no one
You walk hand in hand with treachery ....You embrace it and encourage it
to fill your own needs
You are without morals
Yes, sir............. Yes, sir ....is all you believe, your life is truly empty
Your heart is weak
You are men who speak by the foolish word
Spoken by cowards festered with betrayal
What chance has your family got when it is taught by you ...... A conspirator
in weakness and betrayal
My family has PRIDE they walk with heads held high ...... For it is us,
Our kind who are Gods children ...
Men of TRUTH and HONESTY

The Warrior Within

The bravest of men with the ability to be fair
A mind so sharp, so perfectly balanced
The bite of the warrior as he grits his determined teeth
All else forgotten as his sword leaves its sheath
A man who can decide within the blinking of an eye
To never fear that you may be wrong though be cautious while looking strong
Better to do one thing with all ones might than to half-heartedly attempt many feats
To hold his concentration, be focused and composed
When all around him chaos is crashing down
Nothing sways him, nothing influences him, the decision is his as is the time to unveil it
Always be strong though   he understands the ways of the weak
Every action can be seen from different angles .... The warrior sees them all
He listens more than he speaks .... Listening is the birth of knowledge
Speaking is its death
One hand for giving, one hand for taking
One eye for looking, one eye for seeing

See what you hear

His spoken word is to promise
For no words of fools ever pass his lips
His smile is a rarity
Spurred only by affection
Eyes of sincerity, innocence and truth
He has no prejudices nor can none affect him
He knows only right from wrong
Always without a thought of hesitance
To hesitate is to trust in the ways of others
Trust only in his inner self, it is the only truth you'll ever know
Hear the word of council spoken by friends and foe
Though never heed their advice, advice is weakness
Patronising fools telling the world of their mistakes
Study their faces as they tell you their weaknesses.

Anger

An emotion so strong it corrodes all the rest
Voice is strained from the pain in my chest
We shout and we scream, we hurt those who are close
Damaging the ones who we love the most
It turns you into someone, you didn't want to be
Someone who is blinded, unable to see
Now I am sorry, sorry again
Sorry for causing so much pain
Why don't I think, before I open my mind
Why do I try to be so unkind
Blood flowing fast, I want to destroy
Rip out your soul, take away your joy
Why do I do it, why try to hurt
Why are my words being used as a quirt?
Now I am calm and not like before
Feeling like a fool for my little war
But can I say sorry, will you forgive
Can you show mercy, live and let live
Can you see past, my contrived lies?
Can you now listen to my desperate cries?
I am foolish and stupid, I made myself weak
Now I sorry with tears on my cheek
If I could go back, I would choose my words well
But there is no return, once you are in hell
Cut off my hand, cut off my arm
Give me the strength for me to stay calm
Just remember the way I lived.

The Day is Mine

Today is the day I will make my mark
Today is the day I will join the greats
Everything I have I will lay on the line
Today I face an opponent who does not respect me
I will show him what a mistake he has made
I will strike harder than ever before
I will lay my life before him and see if he shares the same heart
With every blow I will summon my soul
With every step forward I will show him my worth
There will be no surrender
There will be no mercy
I will be ruthless
Strong
I refuse to relent
I refuse to be beaten
My heartbeat will sound like thunder
I will roar like the lion
Let this battle be my legacy
Let this day be the day I am measured
Let this day be the day I join the greats

Reflection

So, the dust has settled and once again I have won
Emotionally I am in pieces
I have gone to that place where only few are brave enough to go
Hung on the cliffs of oblivion
Lowered myself into the clutches of death
Only now can I take a deep breath
Contemplate and sigh as I gasp at my madness
How many more times can escape a glorious death
How many more times can my mind recover from such gamble
Once again I have returned
Again, another piece of my soul has been ripped away
Another piece of my heart has left me
The look of stern on my face is another shade darker
The look in my eyes another degree colder

The Road to Ruin

It is a path we all know
It is a path we all fear
A path with such lure
Just one step and then it's too late
Strange how we choose to ruin our fate
Like Adam and the apple, we know it is wrong
Fooling ourselves we are robust and strong
We choose to be weak, we choose to fail
The lure of wealth is our holy grail
Take another step and we pause for a thought
It doesn't feel right, we know we are caught
Deeper and deeper we soon become
With every step our humanity goes numb
Greed and power, we slowly advance
We are now entrenched and engrossed in the dance
Must keep going, there is no turning back
We're on the road to ruin

Free

I was born into this world chained by circumstance
Born into a way of life not of my choosing
Imprisoned within a body where I was shackled by life
Couldn't break free, no matter how hard I tried.
Now tainted by a mind which is ripped apart
A heart which cries to be free
Am an outlaw or a man who will not kneel down
Am I a monster who will not comply?
How can a man be free?
How can a man live his own life?
I breathe and I live day to day
Yet I question and I doubt
I see life through a mask of un-trust
Looking at everyone with question
Do they love me or love who I am
What am I?
What kind of a man have I become?
I love yet I am afraid to love
I give yet I am wary to give
I trust when I know I should not
A man from a long-lost era
A man who lives life by his heart
I am a dinosaur, lost an age of no romance
Lost in an age of self-importance
When will someone love like I dream?
When will my prayers be answered?
In my past I was a man of the glens
Wind in my hair and freedom in my blood
I made my own rules
I set my own goals
Now it is my curse
Why did I never realise when I was younger?
When will I be free?
When my body is laid to rest

Only then will my soul be free
Only then will I know true peace
My only hope is my sons are spared this legacy
Let them be their own men
Let them live the way they want
I am their father, yet I cannot be their example
It is a pain they should not suffer
A way of life that was mine ...not theirs.
Lord, give me the strength to free them from this bondage
Let them be free
Let them live good
Let them live long and happy
Let them never know the burdens I have carried
I love them with all my heart
Let my suppression, be their freedom
Live my sons live and be free...
Do not remember me

Why Worry

What will happen will just happen
So why spend your days and nights worrying about it
We all try to do the best we can. But still trouble knocks on our door
So, hey! Just let it happen.
Spend today enjoying what you have and not worrying about tomorrow
What can they do anyway/?
Can they take my soul?
Can they take my life?
Only if I give them
I am fed up worrying, tired of trying to second guess all the answers
So damn it! No more will I waste my days fretting and hiding
No more will I try to please those who are my enemy
Do what you want!

My Father

Lived my life under his wing
To me he was everything, my only king
My reason for being, my god and my lord
For him I would die and live by the sword
I have never been me, only the son
Only in his death has my life begun
I yearned for his pleasure, strived for his smile
Scuppered my life and pretended a style
I rose every morning with only one wish
A nod of approval and a fatherly kiss
To me he was everything, my future, my life
The dread of his scowl would cut like a knife
But what of me now, when I am now all alone
Am I worthy or just to sit on his throne
He was a legend, a myth, a man amongst men
Now that I know what I should have known then
He left me alone, to stand on my feet
Told me to fight and not accept defeat
But he should have loved me, for being his son
Not for the man who now all shun
I did what you asked, I followed your ways
Now I am lonely, alone most days
You wanted a prodigy, you wanted an heir
But with all your qualities, you didn't act fair
You steeped me in burdens, handed me the weight
When you should have shown mercy, told me straight
I love you dad, I always will
But you should have gave me the strength to sometimes kneel
What hope do I have now you are gone afar?
How can I live with a heart so scarred?

Truth

An eternity of gratefulness is my reward for the truth
Just one hour of truth, 60 minutes, 60 seconds of pure and innocent
absolute truth
What kind of sensations would it send to my heart?
Will it leave me refreshed or thirsting for more?
Just one tiny hour of truth where everything is clear and full of
understanding
A million years of questions revealed in an hour
A million years' worth of burdens and aches destroyed by the truth

What is the actual meaning of truth?
That which has no questioning
That which has no doubts

Do we ever experience truth................? Pure truth.
Truth bottom line .... Absolute and total

I doubt we ever do...

A Soldiers Doctrine

A Soldiers Doctrine

In a crisis...stay calm
Always strike to kill. A wounded man can still kill you
Wake early and smell the morning, say your prayers and calm your
thoughts,
To be rash will lead to failure,
Cherish and protect your fellow soldiers,
Respect and honour the structure of command,
Carry yourself with dignity and pride,
Show obedience when in battle,
As a man, be the example,
Show mercy when the time arises,
In victory show compassion,
A soldier's voice is soft when not in battle,
He is calm and dignified,
Never disgrace your House or Lord,
Have complete duty to the crown

Swing the sword

If death should come - then make it swift
To be spared of this horror would be god's gift
We fight in the sand, make steps in the mud
Scars in our hearts and covered in blood
We swing our swords using all our might
Smoke and blood hindering our sight
I tread on the bodies of those I call kin
Then question myself for doing such sin
If we win we lose but we must prevail
But will I ever lose this guilt or lose my scowl.

Where have I gone?

Why can I not cry?
What stops me from pain?
Why does death not affect me anymore?
What am I becoming?
I want my feelings back!
I want to know what it feels like to show remorse,
I want to know what it feels like to be a man again,
I am hollow now,
I look at myself in the mirror and I see a stranger
I see empty eyes
I see coldness
I see nothing
God help me...save me from myself.

Choices

When another man barks and another man bites
another man runs and another man fights
When some will shout and some will scream
some will do, some will dream
men of all shapes, mean of all forms
some are rebellious and some reformed
those who say yes and those who say no
Those who are ignorant and others will know
those who take and those who give
some who choose chains while others just live.
those who are strong while others ore meek
some men are quiet while others just speak
men who are calm where others are show haste
some men just eat while others will taste
the world is an arena where some men shine
the world is your oyster but can never be mine

Greed

A man who is content and driven by me
Blind to the world and all who can see
Head in the air brazen and loud
Walking above his own chosen crowd
He seeks to find peace and importance from choice
Only ever interested I hearing his own voice
He walks through the world caring little for his brother
Self-importance ignorant of another
He dreams of more, more than he's got
Blinded by those of which they have not
He has created his kingdom, made his throne
Little does he know he is all on his own
But his pride will not falter, his pride will not bend
Twisted and corrupt, where is the end
He looks down his nose and makes his own claim
Blinded by pride and courted by fame

War

Now pon the time where shivers chill the soul
A twitch on my brow as I look up into the calm night sky
I can hear the sound of calm,
Waiting for the morrow when whistles commence the sound of guns
Rata-tat-tat, then men start to fall
Men who the night before I called them my brother
In the mud and blood, we try to make sense
Yet what words could aptly describe such carnage
I walk over bodies, limbs and shattered dreams
I fall into warm blood which once filled men's hearts
 I feel a thud in my arm which knocks me to the ground
Then the feeling of warmth as my sight turns to crimson
The bang from the impact numbs me for a moment
Before I realise the horror that a bullet found its target
I fall to the ground fearing another round is on its way
Only to see more of my brothers take my place
What bravery they show, what men I stand beside
No matter what I feel I must get to my feet
Together we may find a way to survive this hell
Together we carve our resolve
Together we share a common bond
Together we fight as lions of the British Empire
For King and country flows through our veins
For the regiment and all that went before us
If we fall, then we fall knowing that we join the noblest stock
Go forward and we never stop
Do not shed a tear for us
Hold your head up high and remember us
Be proud of us and know that we are here so you do not have to be
With our sufferance, we give you your freedom
With our pain, we give you peace
We are soldiers
We are men of the empire
Men of nobility
Men of war

Joe Pyle Reg Kray Joe Louis Alex Steen Ron Kray

A still tongue keeps a wise head

**

Don't dabble with the devil unless you are prepared for him to dabble with you.

**

Play with bees then someday you will get stung.

**

A man cannot always be judged by the ways in which those beneath him act.

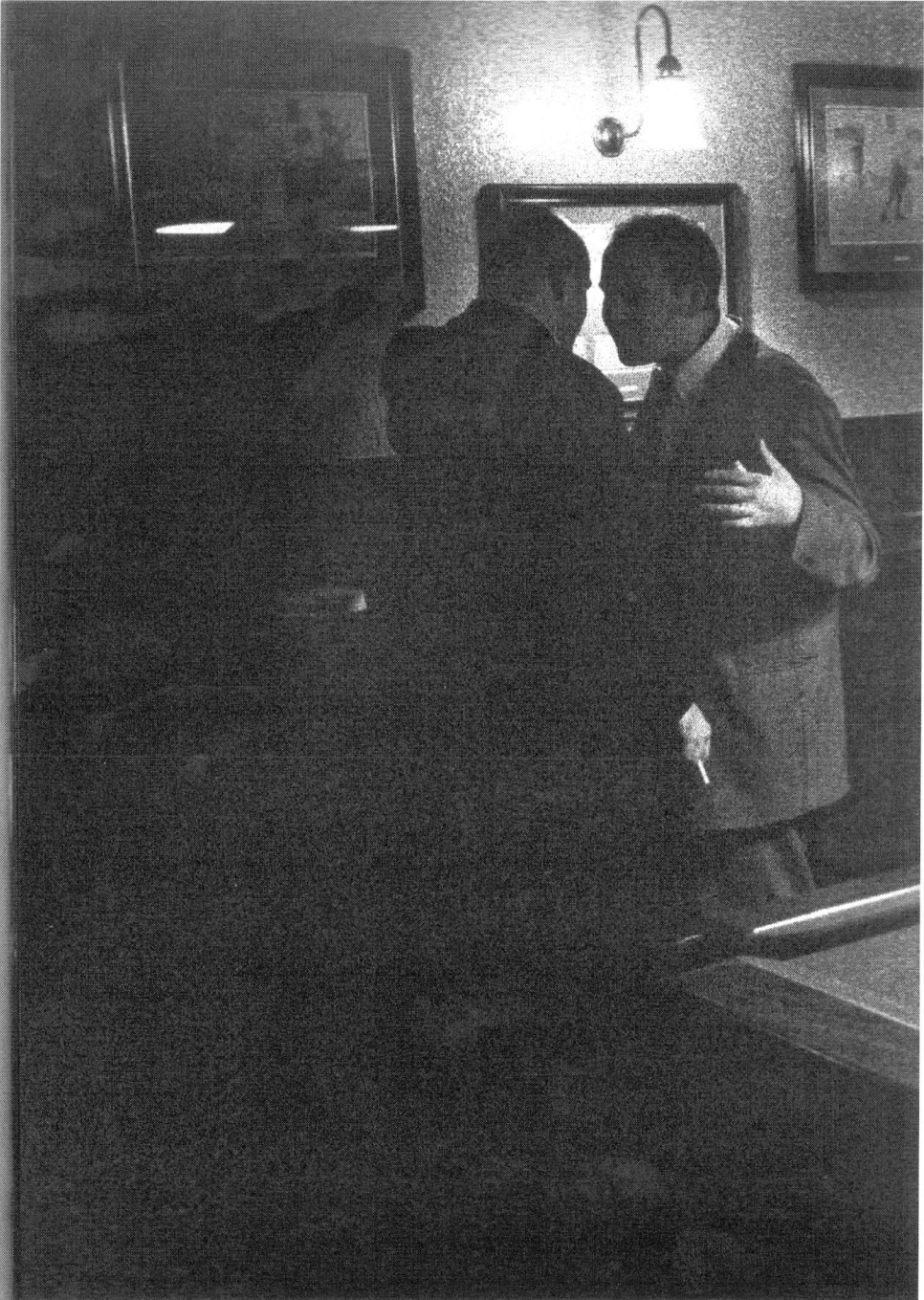

Joe Pyle jnr in the Monday club (Peckham)
credit. Jocelyn Bain Hogg

Ending or the beginning?

Joe Pyle jnr is now one of the most successful professional boxing managers in the UK.

He now spends his time taking care of his family and his boxers, what's next for him?

Like Joe says "You never know just what is around the corner, one day you can be bored stiff and the next day you cannot think straight from work. I keep my options open and live as I have always lived ... day by day! It makes me laugh when people around me hear their phone ring and don't answer. and then they say they cannot be bothered! I just laugh and shake my head as they haven't got my mantra... 'answer the call! You never know it could be a call which changes your life!'"

Trevor Cattouse – Roy Shaw – Joe Pyle Jnr - Deano

Acknowledgements

To some of the people who have shared a big part of this life with me.

Joe Pyle Snr – Ted Pyle – Jean Pyle – Lorraine Pyle – Den Phinbow - Alex Steene – Charlie Richardson – Ronnie Kray – Charlie Kray – Peter Brayham Wilf Pine – Bruce Reynolds – Mitch – Alan – Teddy – Alan Paramasivan - Rod Doll – Dave Thursting - Mike Biggs – Ronnie Biggs – Steve Slater - Paul Ferris – Steven Wraith – Christian Simpson – Rob Davis – Richard Hunt snr & jnr

Eddie Cox – Johnny Edwards – Lewis Edwards – Ricky English – Cream – Marc Carey – Dave Courtney – Brendan McGir – Welsh Phill Davies - Sven Hamer – Gary Sayer – Fred Batt – Brian Harvey - Rob Davis – Baz Allen Johnny Corbett – Richard Mallett - Andy Hollinson – Warren – Alan D - Ade - Johnny Crittenden- Ori Spado – Anthony Spado – Tommy Saulo – Greg Steene – Harry Holland – Tony Lambrianou – John Nash – Jim Nash – Roy Nash – Ronnie Nash – The RoseHill lads – Shawn B – Lady Janet Neaves – Gary C London – and to all of those I can't name because you would get me in bloody trouble x

Joe Pyle aged 19

Joe Pyle Jnr & Snr & Ray Winstone

Joe Pyle Jnr & Mitch Pyle

photo credit Jocelyn Bain Hogg

Joe Pyle Jnr - Tony Lambrianou - Terry Inns

Joe Pyle Snr – Jimmy White – Alan P – Joe Pyle Jnr – Patsy Palmer

Roy Shaw & Joe Pyle Jnr

Joe Pyle Snr & Jnr

Be safe and remember there are
Seven deadly sins....
pride, greed, lust, envy, gluttony, wrath, and sloth...
and
Seven heavenly Virtues
chastity, temperance, charity, diligence, patience, kindness, and humility..,
Choose wisely!

JP Jnr

Joe Pyle snr

Excerpts from the working script for Joe Pyle Snr life story
Written by Joe Pyle jnr

Setting;
Italian restaurant in Mulberry St. New York
Dimly lit with the rain crashing against the window.

JOEY PYLE IN HIS 50'S (RAY WINSTONE)

Joe Pyle is sitting alone at a far table with his back against the wall facing the entrance.
Mario Lanza is playing quietly in the background.
Joe is deep in thought and looking slightly agitated, he looks at his watch and then gazes at the entrance, obviously waiting for someone, someone who is late.
A small set Italian waiter walks over and nervously places some bread and olive oil on the table, joe gives him a slight nod of the head acknowledging his action before reverting his eyes back towards the entrance.
A moment later two Italian wise guys enter the restaurant, they take a brief look around and then give a nod of respect to Joe who they see at the table.
Joe ignores them.
One of the wise guys then turns and opens the door for Joe Pagano, an old and very respected member of the Genovese family who casually enters.
Joey Pyle smiles as he see's old Joe followed by his son Danny arriving, the Paganos quickly walk over to the table where Danny pulls out a chair for his father and apologises to Joe Pyle for being late.
"Hey Joe, we got held up in the tunnel, has the waiter looked after you?"
"That's alright, don't worry about it." Replies Joe Pyle as he turns to old joe noticing the slight embarrassment on his face for being late.

The waiter quickly brings over more bread and three coffees as the men take their seats.
Old Joe smiles at Joe Pyle, it's an endearing friendly smile, a smile that shows his respect and admiration for the man who sits before him.
"How is your troubles back home?" he asks looking concerned.
Joey Pyle as usual hesitates his reply, an old trait where it seems he contemplates every word before he says it.
"It's working itself out."

"That's good, there is nothing worse than when a man cannot return to his home….be with his family and friends." Replies old Joe before leaning forward and lowering his voice.

"That problem in London……is finished."

"He paid?" Joe Pyle asked leaning forward although he knew already the man had paid the money he owed.

"Last night, he settled the debt and paid all the interest…thank you joe." Answered Old joe before leaning back and looking at his son Danny who suddenly produced a large envelope and placed it on the table.

"What's this" Joe Pyle asked as he looked down onto the table.

"It's a thank you." Danny replied.

Joe Pyle winced as he looked at the bulging envelope, he could clearly see it was a bundle of money, he half smiled and the politely leaned back in his chair.

"I didn't do it for money!" he then said quietly.

"Joe you did us a favour; this is our thanks."

Joe Pyle picks up his cigarette's and lights one, he takes a large drag before answering.

"I didn't do it for money; I did it cos we're pals."

"There's a lot of money on that table Joe…take it, treat yourself to something."

"That's not the way we do things….you're a pal and we don't take money from our pals."

Old Joe sighs and half smiles as he shakes his head slightly, he then looks to his son who shrugs as he takes the envelope from the table.

"You London guys, your codes of honour sometimes even humble us!" old Joe says affectionately.

"There must be something we can do for you joey, this is our town and you're our guest." Old joe says.

"What about a broad!. Do you want a broad?" Danny adds which quickly gets a dressing down look from his father.

"There is something." Joe Pyle adds ignoring Danny's outburst.

"What!" old Joe says opening his hands.

"Coney island…..I have always wanted to go to Coney Island."

"Coney fucking island!" Danny replies looking bemused, "It's a fucking ghost town!"

"Yeah, I'd like to look around it, if you could get one of your guys to drive me over there that would be good."

"Okay……we're get someone to take you out there." Old Joe says as he reaches across the table and grabs his hand warmly and smiling broadly.

"When do ya wanna go?" Danny asks.

"Tomorrow would be good."

Old Joe then remembers something

"Listen, a friend of ours has just got out the can and we're having a big homecoming for him on Friday, Tribeca grill, Bobby De Niro's place, why don't you come with us Joe?"

Joe Pyle leans back and takes a sip of his coffee

"Fridays no good Joe, I'm leaving for palm springs on Thursday morning."

"Palm springs! What the fuck is in palm springs." Danny snaps

"The sun, swimming pools and warm weather." Joey Pyle says as he looks at the window where the rain is lashing against it.

"Okay Joe, but do me a favour…. there's a friend of ours out there, a guy called Bobby Milano, look him up when you're there, he will make sure you get whatever you want."

"That's okay Joe."

"Listen, you are under our roof, let us at least make sure the doors are open for you."

"Alright, I'll look him up." Joe replies smiling as he gets to his feet.

The three men shake hands and Danny reminds Joe that someone will pick him up at his hotel at seven to bring him back to the restaurant where a large dinner was planned.

"I'll see ya later." Joe Pyle says as he walks out into the rain to his son Joe jnr waiting outside with an umbrella.

"Alright dad."

"All good, c'mon let's get out of the rain." He replies as they walk quickly over to the chauffeur driven Mercedes.

The two men jump into the back and Joe tells the driver to take them back to the Waldorf.

Young Joe notices his father is deep in thought, "You alright dad?"

Joe smiles at his son and pats his leg, "yeah all good."

"Poxy weather!" young Joe says as he looks out the window.

"Don't worry; we're be by the pool in a couple a days' time."

"ITS LIKE LONDON!" the chauffer suddenly snaps as he turns his window wipers on to full speed.

"They say it always rains in England." He adds as Joe looks out the window.

Joe Pyle looks stoic, he looks out at the tall buildings deep in his own thoughts, thinking of home and the family he misses and loves so much.

'Sinner or saint by Sarah Vaughan is playing on the radio which makes the mood seem more sombre.

Camera to focus on Joe's face as he looks out of the window, he looks sad but strong, in the distance the Brooklyn bridge comes into view which catches Joe's eye. The music gets louder as the camera moves from Joe onto the bridge which suddenly fades into Tower Bridge.

SCENE – LONDON – BOMB SITES AND RUINS - RAY NARRATES OVER SCENES

1949

London is still recovering from WW2. There are bombsites everywhere and life is hard as people struggle on rations. Crime is rampant and is the only way people can get by with a little bit extra.

NARRATION (RAY) (50 seconds – one minute)
Looking back at how things were you might think we had it hard and suppose we did!
But to us things were normal….This was London after the war, battered and bruised yet it was still our home….we never knew any different.
Some kid's earliest memories are sitting on their granddads knee or running in a garden. Mine was hiding down the Angel train station at night while bombs were landing above our heads. I can remember the booms and sometimes the whole ground would shake.
Everyone round where we lived had it hard, it was where the Germans concentrated their bombing, Kings Cross around the docks, we was right in the middle of it and maybe that's why we came out the war without a care.
Life was cheap, we all knew someone who had died in the bombings…….but those who survived, survived with a new attitude…..an attitude where we didn't care and a yearning to get what we thought we deserved.

SCENE - QUIET LONDON STREET- EARLY EVENING
Joey, Johnny, Readsy, Tony and jack walking down the road with Tony carrying a bag full of breaking in tools.
JOHNNY
This ain't gonna be a waste time Joey, this money's definitely gonna be here.
JOEY
(Joey laughs slightly) whatdya think I been working down there all those nights for.
TONY
So you know where everything is then Joe, you know where they keep the money
JOEY
I know everything mate, don't worry we're get a result here.

ROBBERY
The boys climb through the window which Joey had left open where they find the money.

SCENE-JOEY'S BEDROOM
Back at Joey's house where all the boys are looking at all the money on the bed.
(Story from the book!)

NARRATION (RAY)
Once you get a taste of easy money it's very hard to think about getting it any other way. Where we lived there weren't many jobs anyway, some boys went down the docks and broke their backs or tried to get aprentaships in the printing game, but for us that was never gonna be an option. We had tasted the life we wanted….We were hooked and we wanted more.
Over the next few years we robbed everything. We were like a mini crime-wave….anywhere there was money we weren't far away.
Crime in those days wasn't what people call crime today, everyone was doing something, and everyone had to survive.

1954

FADE TO:
EXT. LONDON, EAST END STREET - DAY
The air is very thick with London fog.
The street is packed with a mix of TEDDY BOYS, and guys just mingling around
Joey, in a tailor-made drape suit, Johnny, Readsy and Baldassare, all smartly dressed, emerge from a new, white Mercedes, 1956, 190SL.
Smart black and white shoes get out the car first. A few girls turn and look at Joe who pulls out a comb and combs his hair.
Jailhouse rock by Elvis Presley playing loudly on the car, radio.
The four boys lock the car as everyone about is looking at them, a few people shout out hello and a few girls give smiles as the boys walk towards a snooker hall across the street.
Johnny leads the way but before they get to the entrance Joey pulls his arm gently.
JOEY
Do we really want to get involved with these two?
JOHNNY

pg. 193

What's the matter?
JOEY
We don't need them and we don't need the heat which goes with them.
JOHNNY
What are we in this game for? They said they will pay more money.
JOEY
Alright John, IL go with you on this, but I'm telling ya we don't need them.

NARRATION (RAY)
The Krays twins, even as young boys they demanded fear, everyone spoke about them and most feared them. To us they were just another firm surviving on the streets of London, but we knew it was inevitable that our paths would cross. We had met before me , John, readsy and the twins when we were all banged up together for national service. Even in the nick they were like film stars. People were drawn to them. Maybe it was because they were twins but whatever it was they had a strong charisma. Johnny had got quite close to them when we were locked up. I never had it too much with them as I concentrated on my boxing. A lot of people said Ronnie was the more dangerous, he was registered mad and blew his top over the stupid of things. But for me it was Reg, he was more cunning, he would pull you in and make out you were his pal and then once your guard was down and you didn't expect it he would jump all over ya. It was like in boxing, Ronnie was the punch you saw coming, you had time to stiffen or dodge it but Reg was the punch you never saw, the punch which knocks you out.

SCENE- SNOOKER HALL- SMOKY AND DARK
Inside the snooker hall which is thick with smoke, Reg and Ron are sitting against the bar surrounded by a dozen of their hangers on. Both boys are dressed exactly the same, tailored suits, ties, tie pins and white hankies in their suit pockets. Reggie see's Joe and the boys walk in and to John's slight annoyance walks over to shake Joe's hand first.
REG (talking quiet)
Hello Joe, it's been a long time
JOE
Alright, how are ya
REG then shakes John's hand and the others before he ushers them into the club and into Ronnie's company.

RONNIE

Hello Joe, hows the boxing?

JOEY

Going well Ron, I hear you're not fighting anymore.

Ronnie gives a slight nervous laugh as he looks to his twin

RONNIE

Nah, no more fighting for us, boxing's a mugs game.

Joey nods his head, raises his eyebrows and utters a slight laugh at Ronnie's comment. Johnny quickly intervenes and starts to talk about business

JOHNNY

Alright! We gonna get on with this.

RONNIE

So how many snout do you have?

He asks bluntly which clearly angers Joe at his outburst in front of so many people.

JOEY

Are we gonna go somewhere to talk about this, lot of ears here.

He says as he glances around the dozen or so crowd.

RON

It's alright Joey, there with us.

REG

I heard on the streets you have about five grands worth

Joey just raises his eyebrows and tilts his head as he looks at Reg unimpressed.

JOHNNY

No flies on you Reg, yeah five grands about right.

RONNIE

Look, we can sell them, we're give you four grand, you can have two now and another two tomorrow night.

REG

You got them with you.

JOHNNY

Round the corner Reg, can have em here in about ten minutes.

RONNIE

Alright, go and get them and il get you your two grand!

Johnny looks at Joe and raises his eyebrows, then the four boys walk away for a moment to talk on their own

JOHNNY

What I tell ya, that's a grand more than fat Solly offered us.

JOEY

Yeah it's a good price…..You wanna do business with them John.

JOHNNY

There offering more money mate, they're good money getters…Why not work with them.

Joey looks at his friend and hesitates, it clear he has his reservations but agrees to appease his friend.

JOEY

Alright John, do your deal.

He says before walking back to the twins

JOEY

Alright Ron, we're haveem here in the hour.

Ronnie smiles and nods before looking at one of his crowd and giving him a nod to fetch a bottle of scotch.

RONNIE

Wonderful! Let's have a drink to toast the deal.

Joey smiles but quickly rebuffs his offer of a drink.

JOEY

Not for me Ron, I gotta go training, fighting at the weekend.

RONNIE

Its only one drink Joey, that won't do you any harm.

Joey completely ignores Ron's request and turns to John and Tony

JOE

Il leave this with you then

He says to them before turning back to the twins

JOEY

Alright lads, Johnny's gonna stay with you and sort this out, I'm gonna get away.

22846561R00113

Printed in Great Britain
by Amazon